Improve Your English

Improve Your English

Silvia M. Fernandez

Commonwealth

Improve Your English

Edition : 2025

ISBN 978-81-311-0233-6

Published by **:**
COMMONWEALTH PUBLISHERS (P) LTD.
4831/24, Govind Lane,
Ansari Road, Darya Ganj,
New Delhi - 110002
Ph. : 23272541, 23242541
e-mail : commonwealthpublishers2016@gmail.com

Distributed by :
ARJUN PUBLISHING HOUSE
4831/24, Govind Lane,
Ansari Road, Darya Ganj,
New Delhi - 110002
Ph. : 23272541, 23242541
e-mail : arjunbooks2001@gmail.com

Laser Typesetting by :
Dimple Computers
Delhi

Printed at :
Balaji Digital Press
Delhi

Preface

For several years now English has been accepted in virtually every part of the world as the preferred second language—the language that two people will urn to when they cannot understand each other's language. Moreover, in the era of globalisation, English has emerged almost as first language, it being no longer avoidable in day-to-day activities. As such, a good and thorough knowledge of this language is not only handy, but a requisite to successive and be successful in an age of cut-throat competition.

This book, designed as a language-improvement manual, should serve highly well for those seeking to enhance both their written and verbal skills in English. Incorporating a number of methods and examples to enhance one's vocabulary, grammar and literary skills, the book seeks to provide readers with a veritable list of 'dos' and 'dont's' which should prove to be of great use. Further, it includes innumerable techniques which attempt to test the readers in English usage, particularly in practical situation. The inclusion of various practice exercise should greatly aid in the regard.

Dr. Silvia M. Fernandez

Contents

1

How to Write Good Essays in English

Commonly, essays are written in response to a preprepared question that demands a critical appraisal of the topic at hand. The benefits of writing essays are as follows:

Writing essays :

- consolidates your understanding
- allows you to delve more deeply into a particular subject area
- stimulates your mind by assembling an argument
- gives you practice in using technical or specialist terminology
- enables you to express your thoughts clearly and logically
- encourages you to think and read widely and deeply.

There are several stages in the production of a high quality essay. These are as follows:

- Preparing

- Gathering
- Structuring
- Writing
- Checking & Revising

STAGES IN ESSAY WRITING

The following advice will help you establish what and how you are being asked to write. In preparing your essay you will need to identify the precise subject area that you will be writing about as well as the treatment you will be applying to it.

Ground Rules

Any restrictions in length

Focusing your thoughts into a shorter essay may require more careful consideration than verbose, lengthy ramblings.

Explore the criteria

Have you been given any indication of what will be assessed? What in particular is your tutor looking for in this essay? Can you ask for clarification?

Examine the question

The essay question or title indicates the required approach or treatment. For example, the following question:

> Consider the advantages and disadvantages of introducing peer appraisal into an organisation and justify its use to employees
>
> ... is asking for two different elements, the consideration of the advantages and

disadvantages and then the justification of these to employees.

With every essay question you attempt you will need to identify and decode the key words.

Make it clear for yourself

Write a quick version of what you think you are being asked to do. Rewrite the title or question in your own words. Discuss this with other students or your tutor. Have you understood the question? What areas, if any need clarifying?

Preparing Your Response

Once you have clarified what you have been asked to write about and how you should treat that subject matter, you will need to consider what material should be included in the essay. Start with what you already know, focusing on your own interests and experiences.

Brainstorm your ideas

To brainstorm focus your mind broadly on the topic at hand and let your ideas flow onto the page. Don't make any judgements about relevance at this stage. The aim is to find out how much you already know.

Ask Questions - What don't I know?

Once you have established your existing knowledge you will need to identify the empty areas in your brainstorm and pose these as questions.

- What don't I know?
- What do I need to know?
- What detail would support my argument?

These questions can then form the basis for your information research in the next section.

Gathering Your Information

Based upon your brainstorm questions you will need to identify:

— What sort of information you are looking for, and;

— Where would be the most appropriate place to find it. Preparing your response

Information sources

Remember that there are many different sources of information, including:

— Journals

— Periodicals

— Theses

— Published texts

— CD ROM

— On-line information

— Audio/video

— Your own lecture notes

— The minds of friends and tutors

When gathering information you should remember the following:

— Always search actively

— Don't take too many notes

— Take structured notes

— Keep a record of your sources (Author, publisher, date, page number)

Structuring Your Essay

Now you can put together a plan for your essay based on;

— Your interpretation of the question

— Your personal thoughts and opinions

— The information you have gathered

Put together a logical structure for your essay as follows:

Introduction

Comment upon:

— The subject you will be discussing

— The main points you will be raising

— The treatment you propose to apply

Your introduction should also relate your essay to a wider academic context/discussion.

Main Body

Present your argument in three or four main points.

— Write a paragraph for each main point

— Support your ideas with examples and references

— Develop your argument coherently

— Ensure that your emphasis is balanced

— Avoid stressing your opinion at the cost of more considered reasoning

Conclusion

Summarise your main points in the conclusion.

Sorting Your information

Using your outline plan, sort through the material that you have collected together and priorities this by asking the following questions.

- What is centrally relevant?
- What is partially relevant?
- What is simply irrelevant?

Relate the material to your outline structure. Remember that such information should enhance your argument not dominate the essay. Your tutor is after your opinion and your ability to use theories and sources.

Writing a Draft

It is time now to write a draft of your essay.

Whilst some people feel content with writing a completed version straight off, this is probably inadvisable to most of us. A draft version engages you with your material and allows you to take an overview once it has been completed.

You can then evaluate your draft, making any amendments as you go along. When approaching the first draft of your essay you will probably need to set aside enough time to write it completely without any interruptions. It is important that the thoughts and ideas flow freely throughout the length of the essay. Any significant breaks in concentration might break your stream of thought and ruin this effect.

Setting aside enough time

To check your essay compare it with your original question interpretation, draft outline, and any assessment criteria that have been prepared by your tutor and/or other students.

Writing for Others

When writing for others always remember that someone else has to understand what you say. To do this:

- Write simply and directly
- Limit your sentence length
- Ensure that each paragraph has a focus
- Use clearly labelled pictures if they will save words
- Use sub-headings to define each section
- Take care to acknowledge clearly the work of others
- List the sources you have referred to for other information
- Leave plenty of space for your tutor's comments.

Checking and Revising

Use the Essay evaluation checklist at the end of this section as a prompt to help you evaluate your own essays.

Problem solving

When you have established any problems ask yourself how these could be most easily resolved. Be realistic. It may not always be possible to start again from scratch. If you are having real problems with your writing consult your tutor.

Presentation

Always consider that your essay has to be read and assessed by somebody else. The presentation of your completed essay should be geared towards this. The best presentation is that which is easy to follow, such as clearly used sub-headings or page numbering. Avoid spending too much time on extravagant presentation. Clarity will be more important than impressive graphics.

Tutors spend a lot of time marking many essays at once. Anything that distracts or discourages them from reading your essay in a favourable light, such as illegibility, should be avoided. If people regularly have problems with your handwriting, for example, you may need to consider word processing all of your significant written projects.

Each time you refer to somebody else's thoughts and arguments you need to both identify clearly who you are referring to and where you found this material.

You need to do this whenever you:

- quote somebody else's work directly
- closely summarise a passage from another writer
- draw directly upon somebody else's writing and ideas.

Referencing

To identify a quoted phrase or idea you need to state the author's name in the main text and include this and other details within a list of references elsewhere in the essay. The most common way of identifying a name within the text is to write in brackets the author's name, the year in which the work was produced and the page number of the source text. There are three basic ways of fully acknowledging these ideas outside of the main text:

- *Footnotes*. Numbers after each textual reference matched with numbered acknowledgements at the foot of each page.
- *Endnotes*. Consecutive numbering of references throughout the text matched with consecutively numbered acknowledgements at the end of the essay itself.
- *Included references*. More detail for each reference within the main text which can be picked up through a bibliography at the end.

All acknowledgements should include the author's name, the year or date of publication, the title of the book, article, report etc., the publisher and the place of publication.

Bibliography

You will also need to list all the publications that you have used to help you write your essay whether you have closely referred to them or not. This will give your tutors an idea of how you have set about writing and indicate to other students possible sources of further information. A bibliography should come at the end of your essay, listing each text alphabetically stating the author, date of publication and publisher.

Using Feedback

Your final task when writing an essay is to reflect upon the feedback received from your tutor and/or other students. This may be invaluable in helping you improve your essay writing skills for future work. Essay writing is an invaluable tool in the development of your understanding of your individual discipline area. Through the construction of detailed, reasoned and balanced arguments you consolidate what you have learned and apply key principles and theories in such a way that is both interesting to you and informative to the reader or assessor.

Essay Assessment Checklist

Introduction/Conclusion

- Does my introduction detail what I will be doing and how?
- Does my conclusion summarise my main points and offer some outcome?

Content

- Have I met the demands of the question?
- Have I met the fixed criteria (length etc.)?
- Have I clearly identified my key points?
- Are they presented in a logical sequence?
- Are each of my points supported by sufficient information and examples?

Use of supporting material

- Is the material centrally relevant?
- Does the material endorse or detract from my argument?
- Does the information flow with or disrupt my central argument?

Plagiarism

- What is the ratio of my ideas to the ideas of others?
- Have I distinguished between my ideas and the ideas of others?

Referencing and bibliography

- Have I acknowledged quotations?
- How have I identified the ideas of others within the text?
- Have I fully referenced each quoted phrase or idea?
- Have I included a bibliography listing all of my background reading?

Presentation

- Is there enough space for tutor comments?
- Is my handwriting clear enough?
- Are my sentences short and focused?
- Are each of my paragraphs clearly focused?

COMMON PROBLEMS IN ESSAY WRITING

Relevance

1. Straying off the subject in question is a common problem. There are several simple solutions.
2. Always write out the question accurately and in full on both your notes and your essay script.
3. Plan your essays carefully, consult the wording, and relate each part of your argument to the topic(s) in question.

4. At each stage of the argument, you should keep asking yourself 'Is this relevant?', 'Am I answering the question?', 'Does this relate directly to the subject I have been asked to discuss?'
5. Each paragraph should contain just one idea or topic which is announced in its first sentence. This idea or topic should be directly related to the question or the subject you have been asked to discuss.
6. If you introduce a separate issue in order to illustrate some part of your argument, make sure that you return to the original subject as soon as possible. Part of your discussion should explain why and how this secondary issue is relevant.

Signposting

1. Unless you have been asked to do so, there is no need to 'signpost' your argument.
2. That is, you do not need to use expressions such as:

   'Later in this essay I will be discussing...'

   'Let us now go on to consider...'

   'As I demonstrated earlier...'

   'We will now turn to evaluate another example...'
3. Just state clearly the point of your arguments and leave them to speak for themselves.
4. In a well-planned essay, this progression should

be self-evident from the arrangement of your work.

5. A sound essay plan and a coherent structure will reveal the logic of your argument and the relationship of its parts.
6. Each new topic should be clearly identified or defined as soon as you begin dealing with it. This statement will provide all the indication needed of your intentions.
7. If you wish to some light indication of structure, it is perfectly acceptable to use formulations such as

   'The first reason... The second...'

   'On one hand... on the other...'

   'However, the main argument against this is...'
8. The conventions on signposting may vary slightly from one subject to another. In some of the sciences it is necessary to announce in advance what you will be writing about.

Commenting on the Process

1. Your essay represents the results of your efforts. There is no need to comment on the manner in which you have worked.
2. Your tutor doesn't need to know in what order you assembled your evidence, or what difficulties you encountered during its composition.
3. You might wish to argue that the question raises a certain number of difficulties or crucial issues.

4. You should then go on to discuss their relevance to the subject in question, and maybe even suggest some answers to them.

Posing Questions

1. Do not present your argument in the form of questions.
2. Remember - you are supposed to be answering a question.
3. Avoid formulations such as:

   Was she so overwhelmed at the thought of a 'new brave' husband that she shot him? In considering his cowardice, had Macomber removed his weapon - his weakness?

Your Own Argument

1. Do not use quotation from the text as a substitute for your own argument.
2. That is, don't present your answer to the question as a mixture of your own remarks, woven together with quotations.
3. Here is an example:

   The poem describes a journey 'from rich industrial shadows' through crowded urban environments to a place of 'loneliness' where 'silence stands/like heat'.

Referencing

1. Quotations from a text should be followed by page references - as in the following example:

   These literary devices include simile, such as the

description of the lion as 'like some super-rhino' (p.94) and the...

2. You should not include the reference as part of your text, as in the following example:

   These literary devices include simile, such as the description of the lion on page ninety-four when it is described as 'like some super-rhino' and the other instance on page fifty-six when it is...

Creating Structure

1. Essays should have a clear structure. This should be created in a firm essay plan.
2. Good structure is a persuasive or logical sequence of the parts in an essay.
3. The order of parts is often determined by the nature of the subject. This order might be created by:
   - logical progression
   - increasing significance
   - equal significance
   - chronological order
   - narrative sequence
   - category groupings
4. You can generate the parts of your essay by deciding which topics you will cover in your answer.
5. Each of these topics should be discussed separately —usually in at least one paragraph on its own.
6. If there is no natural order for your topics, you could deal with the smaller, less important items

first. This leaves the larger, more important issues until the end of the essay.

ESSENTIAL STEPS OF ESSAY WRITING

When you write an essay, you are doing more than conveying facts and information; you multiply yourself as a writer and attempt to gain some height, like jumping on a trampoline, catching the gist of what others have been feeling about a topic and then clarifying it for them. An essay has a particular slant, a seasoned person behind it capable of simulating the mind's own processes in a murky and incongruous world. Begin with contem-plation about purpose, situation, and audience; this gives you balance. But essays also have a cutting edge—the facts and information are going to be eclipsed, for what lives in art is spirit, not factuality.

Writers, like scientists, pay attention to details, cultivate a talent for observation. A "value claim" in essay writing is a kind of hypothesis based on the data observed. What do the facts mean? This is where essays begin. Essays, however, have another key square peck that fits awkwardly into the absolute roundness of science—sometimes essayists make leaps of logic or super logic that work a bit like magic.

Even though some author is trying to tell us that the world is flat, "we might want to listen to him elaborate on the fringes of his premise, because the bristle of his narrative and what he's seen intrigue us." This is the bard tradition. The writer tells his audiences something they may not believe or want to believe, but they continue to respond to his spirit as a bibliophile and a writer.

When we think of academics, however, we take essay writers into account in different ways than we do writers of poetry. Poets can sing the blues and travel the wasteland, but if an essayist does the same, without regard for the realm of reality, he queers his legacy. He is supposed to be the voice of reason, he is an advocate for civilisation.

An essay also fits the times, suits the age of reconsideration. Essayists, in dealing with present tense, are stuck with the nuts and bolts of what's going on. A good essay is driven by the momentum of inquiry, searching out a point, struggling with the here and now, the world we have. The fracases they get into are often on behalf of democracy and always zestful.

An essay can have many purposes, but the basic structure is the same no matter what. You may be writing an essay to argue for a particular point of view or to explain the steps necessary to complete a task. Either way, your essay will have the same basic format. If you follow a few simple steps, you will find that the essay almost writes itself. The essential steps of essay writing is given below.

1. *Research*: Begin the essay writing process by researching your topic, making yourself an expert. Utilise the internet, the academic databases, and the library. Take notes and immerse yourself in the words of great thinkers.
2. *Analysis*: Now that you have a good knowledge base, start analysing the arguments of the essays you're reading. Clearly define the claims, write out the reasons, the evidence. Look for weaknesses of logic, and also strengths. Learning

how to write an essay begins by learning how to analyse essays written by others.

3. *Brainstorming*: Your essay will require insight of your own, genuine essay-writing brilliance. Ask yourself a dozen questions and answer them. Meditate with a pen in your hand. Take walks and think and think until you come up with original insights to write about.
4. *Thesis*: Pick your best idea and pin it down in a clear assertion that you can write your entire essay around. Your thesis is your main point, summed up in a concise sentence that lets the reader know where you're going, and why. It's practically impossible to write a good essay without a clear thesis.
5. *Outline*: Sketch out your essay before straightway writing it out. Use one-line sentences to describe paragraphs, and bullet points to describe what each paragraph will contain. Play with the essay's order. Map out the structure of your argument, and make sure each paragraph is unified.
6. *Introduction*: Now sit down and write the essay. The introduction should grab the reader's attention, set up the issue, and lead in to your thesis. Your intro is merely a buildup of the issue, a stage of bringing your reader into the essay's argument.
7. *Paragraphs*: Each individual paragraph should be focused on a single idea that supports your thesis. Begin paragraphs with topic sentences, support assertions with evidence, and expound

your ideas in the clearest, most sensible way you can. Speak to your reader as if he or she were sitting in front of you. In other words, instead of writing the essay, try *talking* the essay.

8. *Conclusion*: Gracefully exit your essay by making a quick wrap-up sentence, and then end on some memorable thought, perhaps a quotation, or an interesting twist of logic, or some call to action. Is there something you want the reader to walk away and do? Let him or her know exactly what.
9. *MLA Style*: Format your essay according to the correct guidelines for citation. All borrowed ideas and quotations should be correctly cited in the body of your text, followed up with a Works Cited (references) page listing the details of your sources.
10. *Language*: You're not done writing your essay until you've polished your language by correcting the grammar, making sentences flow, incoporating rhythm, emphasis, adjusting the formality, giving it a level-headed tone, and making other intuitive edits. Proofread until it reads just how you want it to sound. Writing an essay can be tedious, but you don't want to bungle the hours of conceptual work you've put into writing your essay by leaving a few slippy misppallings and pourly wordedd phrazies.

Step 1: Research

Assuming you've been given a topic, or have narrowed it sufficiently down, your first task is to research this topic. You will not be able to write intelligently about a topic you know nothing about. To discover worthwhile insights, you'll have to do some patient reading.

Read light sources

When you conduct research, move from light to thorough resources to make sure you're moving in the right direction. Begin by doing searches on the Internet about your topic to familiarise yourself with the basic issues; then move to more thorough research on the Academic Databases; finally, probe the depths of the issue by burying yourself in the library. Make sure that despite beginning on the Internet, you don't simply end there. A research paper using only Internet sources is a weak paper, and puts you at a disadvantage for not utilising better information from more academic sources.

Write down quotations

As you read about your topic, keep a piece of paper and pen handy to write down interesting quotations you find. Make sure you write down the source and transcribe quotations accurately. I recommend handwriting the quotations to ensure that you don't overuse them, because if you have to handwrite the quotations, you'll probably only use quotations sparingly, as you should. On the other hand, if you're cruising through the net, you may just want to cut and paste snippets here and there along with their URLs into a Word file, and then later go back and sift the kernels from the chaff.

With print sources, you might put a checkmark beside interesting passages. Write questions or other thoughts in the margins as well. If it's a library book, use post-it notes to avoid ruining the book. Whatever your system, be sure to annotate the text you read. If reading online, see if you can download the document, and then use Word's Reviewing toolbar to add notes or the highlighter tool to highlight key passages.

Take a little from a lot

You'll need to read widely in order to gather sources on your topic. As you integrate research, take a little from a lot — that is, quote briefly from a wide variety of sources. This is the best advice there is about researching. Too many quotations from one source, however reliable the source, will make your essay seem unoriginal and borrowed. Too few sources and you may come off sounding inexperienced. When you have a lot of small quotations from numerous sources, you will seem — if not be — well-read, knowledgeable, and credible as you write about your topic.

Researching on the internet

While the Internet should never be your only source of information, it would be ridiculous not to utlise its vast sources of information. You should use the Internet to acquaint yourself with the topic more before you dig into more academic texts. The Internet contains some 550 billion web pages. Google is a powerful search engine, but it only reaches about 5 billion of those pages — less than one percent! When you search the Internet, you should use a handful of different search engines. The Academic Search Engines above specialise in delivering material more suitable for college purposes, while the Popular Search Engines help locate information on less academic topics. Whatever your topic, use a *variety* of search engines from both menus. Once you go beyond Google, you will begin to realise the limitlessness horizons of the Internet.

With all the returns from your searches, you'll doubtless pull in a bundle of sites, and like a fisherman on a boat, your job will be to sort through the trash. The degree of professional design and presentation of a site should speak somewhat towards the content. Sites with black backgrounds are usually entertainment sites, while those with white backgrounds are more information based. Sites with colorful and garish backgrounds are probably made by novice designers. Avoid blog pages (online journals). Avoid "free-essay" pages. Avoid pages where there are multiple applets flashing on the screen.

If you're getting too many hits, enter more keywords in the search box. If you aren't getting enough hits, enter fewer keywords in the searchbox. Also try inputting the same concept but in different words and phrases. Overture has a keyword search suggestion tool that lets you know what the most popular search strings are for the concept you're searching for. Search Engine Watch also has a useful tutorial on how to enter search strings, explaining how to add '+' and '-' and quotation marks to get more accurate results.

Many search engines have advanced tabs that help you search with more detail. Google, for example, has an advanced search option that greatly increases accuracy of returns, though few use it.

Finally, know that some search engines specialise in specific types of content, so if you don't have much success with one search engine, try another.

While it's fun to surf the net and discover new sites with information relevant to your topic, don't limit yourself to the Internet. By and large the Internet, because it is a medium open to publication by all, can contain some pretty sketchy information. If your essay is backed by research from "Steve and Kim's homepage," "Matt's Econ Blog," and "teenstuffonline," your essay won't be as convincing as it would be with more academic journals. Academic journals and books have better research, more thorough treatment of the topics, a more stable existence, and ultimately more persuasive power. Don't substitute Eddy Smith's "Summer Vacation to the Middle East" for Edward Said's *Orientalism.*

Academic databases and libraries

Almost every college subscribes to a list of academic databases where more specialised, academic essays can be found. If you are an AUC student, go to the AUC Library Homepage and choose Electronic Resources to survey the 80+ academic databases that AUC subscribes to. Each of these databases specialises in a different kind of information.

A common misconception among students is that the library is full of old, out-of-date, musty books – probably none from this century – and therefore any books found there would be so out of step with the current discussion on the topic that the books, and any effort to retrieve them, would be utterly useless.

Fortunately, all libraries have acquisitions departments with specialists from different fields of scholarship who constantly order up-to-date books on the contemporary issues in almost all fields. As a result, most libraries have books on all issues at least within the last ten years or so. So unless you're writing about something totally new, chances are a book has been written on it, and most likely that book is waiting for you in the library.

Another misconception many students have is that even if they were to see a book listed on the electronic catalogues, it would be too much of a hassle to physically go to the library, hike the stairs, take elevators perhaps, wander among the stacks and corridors, skim through eternal Library of Congress call numbers, and so on.

While it is true that the physical exertion required (i.e., walking) to find the book is more than that required to click a mouse, once you find the book, it requires less energy to progress through the information than it does to fight the endless screens, non-linear progressions, and specious content on the Internet. In contrast, books are well-organised, logically progressive texts that usually contain abundant research, are written by scholars, and will provide excellent evidence for your essay.

The Internet is full of everything from porno to CIA reports, and it's all jumbled together like paint splattered on a wall. You'll have to sort through it like a homeless man foraging for food in a dumpster. Think about how nice it would be instead to read a chapter from a book while lying in bed.

Because books are so thorough and long (it may have taken the author years to write it, as opposed to an online article, which might have been written in under an hour), you have to learn to skim. Skim the table of contents to see if there is a chapter that is relevant. Read the introduction and the first pages of several chapters to see if the information is really what you're looking for.

Since you will still need to cite from a variety of sources, don't spend too long immersed in the same book. Take a little information from a lot of different books — from an author here, an author there. It might be a good idea to photocopy the necessary pages rather than cart around a backpack full of books.

The more you spend time researching in the library, the more you will come to see what a sanctuary the library can be. The loud, noisy traffic of the streets outside is blocked out as you sit comfortably surrounded by thousands of insightful books on important topics throughout the ages. A library can be a sanctuary to you — a place to study, a place to escape your friends or other obligations, a refuge of peace and quiet. A good library is the heart of any academic institution, and the more time you spend in it, the more it will feel like hallowed ground.

Step 2. Analysis

As you research your topic, you will naturally be analysing the arguments of different authors. In contrast to more popular reading, in the academic world, authors must supply copious amounts of evidence and nuanced reasoning in order persuade other scholars of their ideas. To enter the scholar's "gladiator arena," you will need to understand the principles of argument. Both analysing an argument and coming up with your own will require careful thought.

An argument consists of two main components: a claim, and reasons for that claim. Neither a claim without reasons, nor reasons without a claim, is an argument. Only when one leverages particular reasons to make a claim from those reasons do we say that an "argument" is taking place. When analysing an argument of any text, or creating one of your own, first identify the main claim and then locate all the reasons for it. The claim is the controversial, debatable assertion of the essay, while the reasons offer the explanations and evidence of why the claim is true. Once you have the argument mapped out, assess the reasoning. Ask yourself the following questions to help you identify weaknesses of logic:

(1.) Is there an alternative explanation that is possible? An alternative explanation is a different reason for the same claim. Probing the alternative explanations or reasons for a claim is an excellent way to open up weaknesses in the author's logic.

Example: "John was late because he obviously doesn't care about the class." (An alternative explanation for John's lateness could be that he got in a car wreck, and therefore couldn't make it on time to class, not that he doesn't care about it.)

(2.) Is the evidence presented sufficient? Evidence refers to the support given for a claim. This support may be in the form of facts, statistics, authoritative quotations, studies, observations, experiences, research, or other forms of proof.

Example: "John was late because he has Alzheimer's disease, and according to the American Medical Association, Alzheimer's patients frequently forgot who and where they are" (Jones 65).

(3.) What assumptions do the reasons rest on? An assumption is what one takes for granted to be true, but which actually may not be true. All arguments rest on some common assumptions. This common ground makes it possible for two people to have a dialogue in the first place, but these assumptions, because they are based on groundless ideas, make for a "sweet spot" of attack in argument.

Example: "John was late because his previous class is on the far side of campus." Either/Or: Narrowing the options to just two extremes when in actuality more options exist.

(4.) Does the writer commit any logical fallacies? Fallacies are commonly committed errors of reasoning. Being awarè of these fallacies will help you see them more abundantly in the texts you read. Although there are probably at least a hundred different fallacies, the following six are the most common:

- Hasty Generalisation
- Faulty Cause and Effect
- Fallacy of Authority
- Slippery Slope

— Non Sequitar
— Either/Or

Step 3: Brainstorming

Brainstorming is the art of thinking critically to discover original, hidden insights about a topic. Assuming you've done a fair amount of research, you should now have a solid base of concepts to play around with for an essay. The task is now to stand on the shoulders of the scholars you've read and find something original to say about the topic. It is not enough to regurgitate what they have said. You must go beyond them to propose an original idea. Your paper should expose some new idea or insight about the topic, not just be a collage of other scholars' thoughts and research – although you will definitely rely upon these scholars as you move toward your point.

Since the days of Aristotle, a variety of "invention techniques" or "heuristics" have been used for coming up with ideas. Depending on your topic, some invention techniques may work better than others. The overall goal when using any method is to discover unique ideas that take you and your reader beyond the obvious. The following wheel briefly describes nine of the most common methods for finding ideas. After reading the brief descriptions of each technique, download the Brainstorm Now file (a Word document), and begin brainstorming by answering the questions asked you.

Step 4: Thesis

After researching, analysing, and brainstorming, you

should have an worthwhile insight to write about. Now it's time to convert that worthwhile insight into a polished thesis statement, which will then guide and shape the rest of the essay.

The thesis acts as the main claim of your paper, and typically appears near the end of the introduction. Unless you have a compelling reason to relocate the thesis from the traditional place, put it at the end of your introductory paragraph. Readers anticipate and read closely your thesis, and they want to find a polished statement there. The thesis expresses in one concise sentence the point and purpose of your essay.

Make it arguable

Your thesis must make an arguable assertion. To test whether your assertion is arguable, ask yourself whether it would be possible to argue the opposite. If not, then it's not a thesis -- it's more of a fact. For example:

— *Not arguable*: "Computers are becoming an efficient mechanism for managing and transmitting information in large businesses."

— *Arguable*: "Heavy use of computers may disrupt family cohesion and increase divorce in society."

Be specific

The thesis must also be specific. Avoid broad, vague generalisations. Your thesis should include detail and specificity, offering the reader the why behind your reasoning.

— *Poor specificity*: "We should not pass the microchip bill."

- *Good specificity*: "Because the microchip insert causes serious health hazards such as cancer and brain tumours to those who use it, the microchip should not be passed."

Avoid lists

If your thesis consists of a long list of points, your essay will most likely be superficial. Suppose you had six reasons why WebCT should be adopted in college courses. Instead of trying to cover so much ground in your essay, narrow your focus more to give greater depth to fewer ideas, maybe discussing two or three points instead.

Long lists result in shallow essays because you don't have space to fully explore an idea. If you don't know what else to say about a point, do more brainstorming and research. However, if you're arguing a longer paper, and really need to cover this much ground, still avoid the list in your thesis—just give the reader a general idea of your position, without being so specific.

Example of a list: "The microchip bill biologically damages the health of children, invades the privacy of independent teenagers, increases crime, turns children against their parents, induces a sense of robotry about the individual, and finally, may result in the possible takeover of the government."

Narrower focus: "By surgically inserting circuitry similar to cell phone devices that has been known to cause headaches and fatigue, the microchip biologically endangers the health of children."

Follow an "although... actually" Format

The "although... actually" format is one of the most

effective ways of finding something original and controversial to say. In effect, you are telling someone that what he or she thought to be previously true really isn't. You're saying, Hey, you thought X? Well, you're wrong. Really, it's Y! Whenever you look beyond the obvious and give readers something new to consider, you're going to get their attention. Nothing works better than this "although... actually" format to set you up in delivering an insight.

Step 5: Outline

Can you imagine a construction manager working on a skyscraper without a set of blueprints? No way! Similarly, writers construct essays using sets of blueprints or outlines to guide them in the writing process. Of course writers don't have to use outlines, but the effect is about the same as a construction worker who "freebuilds."

Drawing up an outline allows you to think before you write. What use is there in writing the entire paper only to realise that, had you done a little more planning beforehand, you would have organised your essay in an entirely different way? What if you realise later, after free-writing the essay, that you should have omitted some paragraphs, restructured the progression of your logic, and used more examples and other evidence? You can go back and try to insert major revisions into the essay, but the effect may be like trying to add a thicker foundation to a building already constructed.

The outline allows you to think beforehand what you're going to write so that when you do write it, if you've done your planning right, you won't have to do as much rewriting.

Make Your Points Brief

When you construct your outline, keep it brief. The titles, headings, and points in your outline should be about one line each. Remember that you are only drawing an outline of the forest, not detailing each of the trees. Keep each line under a dozen words. If you can't compress your point into a one-liner, you probably don't have a clear grasp of what you're trying to say.

When you describe the point of each paragraph, phrase the point in a mini-claim. If the point of a paragraph is that *soft drugs should be legal because they are relatively harmless*, don't just write "soft drugs" as the point of the paragraph in your outline — it's too brief and vague. Instead, write "drugs should be legal b/c soft drugs are harmlessl." This description is still brief, as it should be (one line or less), but it makes a claim that gives it purpose in the outline.

Appropriate arrangement

Drawing up an outline allows you to see at a glance how each of the paragraphs fits into the larger picture. When looking at your paragraphs from this perspective, you can easily shift around the order to see how a reorganisation might be better. Remember that each paragraph in the essay should support the position or argument of your paper.

As you're shifting paragraphs around (maybe like you would a Rubic's cube), you will probably begin to wonder what the best arrangement really is. In general, put what you want the reader to remember either first or last, not in the middle. Studies in rhetoric have shown the readers remember least what is presented in the middle of an essay. Hence, the middle is where you should probably put your weaker arguments and counter arguments.

Some writers urge a climactic arrangement, one that works up to your strongest point, which is delivered as a kind of grand finale. Another successful arrangement is the inductive argument, in which you build up the evidence first, and then draw conclusions. A problem-solution format involves presenting the problem first and then outlining the solution — this works well for some topics because it is a soft version of the scientific method. Whatever your choice, choose an arrangement that presents a clear, logical argument.

Step 6: Introduction

The first goal in your introduction is to grab the reader's attention. Wake him or her up and generate some interest about the topic. To grab the reader's attention, you might present...

— an interesting fact

— a surprising piece of information

— an exciting quotation

— an intriguing paradox

— an explanation of an odd term

— a short narrative/anecdote (not fiction)

— a provocative question

Jump right into the issue

In a short essay, a lengthy introduction is hardly

needed. After getting the reader's attention, just jump right into the issue and begin directly, perhaps describing a specific, concrete situation — presumably the context of the problem you're exploring. Avoid beginning your essay with broad statements or bland generalisations such as "X is becoming an issue... " or "Throughout time man has wondered...." Do not begin so broad and general that the first several sentences could fit nearly any essay in the world.

Present your thesis

The entire introduction should lead toward the presentation of your arguable assertion, or thesis, whereby you take a stand on the issue you are discussing. Deliver your thesis at the end of the introduction so that your reader knows what general position you will take in your essay. You don't need to spell out all the nitty gritty details of your thesis in the introduction, particularly if it would be bulky and unintelligible to the reader who lacks all the ensuing reference and context, but you should give the reader a good idea of what your argument is.

Step 7: Paragraphs

Singular focus

Each paragraph should have a clear, singular focus to it. If there is an overriding error students make in writing essays, it is shifting topics within the same paragraph, rather than continuing to develop the same idea they began with. A paragraph is a discrete unit of thought that expands one specific idea, not three or four. If you find yourself shifting gears to start a new topic, begin a new paragraph instead.

Someone once compared the beginning of a new paragraph to the changing angle of a wall. When the angle of the wall changes, a new wall begins. Let your paragraphs be like that wall: running straight along a certain angle, and beginning anew when the angle changes.

Begin with a topic sentence

Nothing will help you keep a tighter focus on your paragraphs than topic sentences. A topic sentence is generally the first sentence of the paragraph, and it describes the claim or point of the paragraph, thus orienting the reader to the purpose of the paragraph. When you use topic sentences, your reader will invariably find it easier to follow your thoughts and argument. The entire paragraph is focused around the stated topic sentence. Additionally, headings are used to make it even clearer and easier to follow. If you're writing a long research essay, you might consider using headings.

Develop the idea

Invariably students shift topics and lose focus within their paragraphs because they do not know how to adequately develop their ideas. They usually know the paragraph needs to be longer, but they don't know how to expand their idea to fill that length. Indeed a paragraph should be at least half a page long, but usually no more than one page. How, then, if you don't have enough to say, do you fill that paragraph length? Instead of broadening the focus, which will only be another form of topic shifting, try implementing these techniques for development:

— illustrate your idea with examples

- give an authoritative quotation
- anticipate and respond to counter arguments
- back your ideas with more evidence
- offer another perspective to the idea
- brainstorm more insights about the idea
- elaborate on causes/effects, definitions, comparison /contrasts

Step 8: The conclusion

If your essay was long and complex, sometimes difficult to follow, in the conclusion you'll want to recap your ideas in a clear, summarising manner. You want your readers to understand the message you intended to communicate. However, if your essay was short and simple, don't insult your readers by restating at length the ideas they already understand. Strike a balance according to what you feel your readers need. In a short essay (600 words or less), any recapitulation should be brief (about 2 sentences), and rephrased in a fresh way, not just cut and pasted from the thesis.

Leave a memorable impression

It's not enough just to restate your main ideas — if you only did that and then ended your essay, your conclusion would be flat and boring. You've got to make a *graceful* exit from your essay by leaving a memorable impression on the reader. You need to say something that will continue to simmer in the reader's minds long after he or she has put down your essay. To leave this memorable impression, try...

- giving a thought-provoking quotation
- describing a powerful image
- talking about consequences or implications
- stating what action needs to be done
- ending on an interesting twist of thought
- explaining why the topic is important

Keep it short

Keep your conclusion short, probably ten lines or less, and avoid fluff. You're just trying to make a clever exit, and presumably all the really important points have been made previously in your essay. You should not introduce any totally new ideas in the conclusion; however, you should not merely repeat your thesis either. This situation – not presenting anything new, and neither just sticking with the old – at first seems to be a paradox.

Step 9: MLA Style

When using ideas or phrases from other writers in your own essay, you must correctly cite in your text exactly where the ideas or phrases come from. Correctly identifying these ideas and phrases is called "in-text citation," and the page at the end of your essay listing the sources you used is called a "Works Cited" page.

Different disciplines follow different style guides for in-text citation and Works Cited pages, but in most writing courses, because they fall under the humanities discipline, MLA (Modern Language Association) Style is used. Although there are many details and rules about incorporating research into your essay, the following five basic principles will help you correctly ingetrate sources in your essay.

1. Make sure all authors cited in the body of your essay also appear on the Works Cited page. If you quote Jones, Smith, and Johnson in your essay, these three authors should appear with full documentation on the Works Cited pagel. Don't forget them. Likewise, all the authors or sources listed in the Works Cited page should appear in the body of your essay. There should be no sources listed on the Works Cited page that were not cited in your actual essay.
2. Only quote catchy or memorable phrases or sentences. If the source you're quoting is unremarkable and dry in its expression or opinion, don't bring that unremarkable, dry text into your own writing as well. Paraphrase this material instead, and follow up your paraphrase with the author's name in parentheses. Only quote catchy, memorable, quotable phrases, and keep the quotations short – one or two lines usually. In general you want to quote sparingly and preserve your own voice.
3. Don't rely too much on the same source. If you have four or five quotes from the same author, your reader will eventually just desire to read that author instead. Too much quoting also compromises your own voice and sense of authority about the issue. Rather than limiting your research to one or two authors, draw upon a wide variety of sources, and quote only snippets from each. Having variety will ensure that you are well read in the subject and that

you've examined the issue from multiple perspectives.

4. Follow up your quotations with commentary, interpretation, or analysis. Avoid just dropping in the quotation and then immediately moving on, assuming the reader fully understands the meaning, purpose, and application of the quotation just presented. You almost always should comment on the quotation in some way, even if your commentary is a simple reexplanation of what the quotation means. Remember that you're taking the quotation from an article you've read, but the reader only gets a glimpse of that whole article and lacks the context that you have, so it might be more difficult for the reader to understand it. Because the essay is supposed to represent your ideas, not just those of another, you must find some way to comment or analyse what you summarise or quote.
5. Use signal phrases to introduce your quotations. A signal phrase is a clause before the quotation that identifies the author. Signal phrases are essential to create a bridge between your own voice and that of another you are incorporating into your essay. If you identify the author in the signal phrase, don't also identify author in parentheses following the quotation. Once is enough.

Step 10: Language

According to Truman Capote, "The greatest pleasure of writing is not what it's about, but the music the words make." As you edit the language of your essay, you are trying to make music out of the words.

In this step the content of your essay should be solid. If the idea itself needs discarding, you shouldn't be tweaking the language; it would be a waste of time working on transitions if the organisation and structure of your essay were in need of repair. Hence editing the language of your essay comes last. Here you are putting polish on a shoe that has already been sewn.

Editing the language can be tedious, but it is essential. You've got to proofread your essays dozens of times to catch all the rough spots and language errors. As you proofread you will be checking for misspellings, poor mechanics, bad grammar, awkward word flow and numerous other linguistic details that you can improve. Proofreading the language may take hours as you attempt to polish your language to the point that it is pleasing to read and has literary style.

Give your eyes rest

The more you read your essay, the more blind you become to it. Soon you stop reading the words on the page and only begin reading what's in your mind, which you falsely transpose onto the page. The actual letters could be Hebrew, or Greek, for all it matters at that point.

Don't keep reading hour after hour until your mind registers the entire text at a glance, without seeing the details. What you must do is rest your eyes; take a break. Give yourself a day or two between revisions. When you come back to your essay with fresh eyes and a renewed perspective, you will see with added clarity all the rough phrasings and strange ideas that your eyes once glided over.

Know what to look for

You can read your essay a thousand times over, but if you don't know what you're looking for, you will probably miss all the errors you're attempting to find. If you're going to work hard, make sure you're putting all your energy to a productive use. Know what to look for when you proofread.

There are twelve areas to look for: logic, evidence, development, focus, structure, unity, integration, in-text citation, works cited, grammar, clarity, style. Check off each category as you examine your essay. Another help for proofreading is to ask yourself the same questions in the Peer Review, conducting instead a "self-review." Finally, be sure to use the spell-checker and grammar-checker in Word.

Don't plagiarize

You might want to ask a friend to read over your essay and give suggestions for change. This is usually advantageous. Some students, however, perhaps feeling pressure to bring their language level up to a more fluent, "A" level, might ask their friends to go beyond a few simple suggestions and instead to heavily edit or rewrite the language of their paper.

While it is generally okay for another to get *some* feedback from others on ideas and language, your friend or family member cannot take upon the role of an editor, changing your sentences and thoughts to reflect a linguistic and analytical level that is not yours and which is beyond your ability. Passing off another's language as your own – even if the ideas remain original to your own mind – is considered plagiarism. Your work must be your own, and that includes the language and style, not just content.

Knowing that the work is your own, and that it represents your highest level of performance, you will feel a sense of achievement and personal growth that perhaps you have not experienced before. Each essay should seem to you that it is your best work to date. Only when you feel this way is the paper done.

Clarity

Few techniques add more clarity to your writing than well-formed topic sentences. Topic sentences usually appear at or near the beginning of each paragraph and tell the reader what the topic of the paragraph will be. Using topic sentences to "signpost" your meaning will orient the reader and help him or her follow comfortably along your path of thought.

You will discover that when a writer uses topic sentences, you can skim the entire essay and still understand the main points. The next time you read a long essay, try reading only the first one or two sentences of each paragraph. You will rarely be lost or confused if the topic sentences make clear what the purpose of each paragraph is.

Make clear transitions

Transitions act as bridges between your paragraphs. Since each paragraph offers a distinct thought, you need to connect these two distinct thoughts in some logical way for the reader. The transitions supply the logic of how two paragraphs connect, how one idea leads to the next, or how the two are related. Don't make the reader guess how one paragraph relates to the other. The following are some common patterns for transitions:

– Not only is vegetarianism unhealthy for the human body, vegetariarism also creates an excess of pesticides in the environment.
– In addition to problems of obesity, America's youth also suffer from increasing amounts of psychological stress.
– Besides violating the right to privacy, the microchip also puts children at danger in the even of information-hacking.

Omit needless words

"Omit needless words!" "Omit needless words!" This was the constant advice, says E.B. White, of his former professor, William Strunk. White says Strunk would occasionally grab a student by the lapels and shout this phrase several times, but then be almost restricted from elaborating more for fear of violating the very principle he was teaching. *Omit needless words, write with concision, make your sentences succinct, cut out the fat, remove the deadwood, make every word pull its own weight* — these common phrases are all intended to convince students to streamline their prose with more efficiency and power by removing unnecessary words.

In Strunk's own words, "Vigorous writing is concise. A sentence should contain no unnecessary words, a paragraph no unnecessary sentences, for the same reason that a drawing should have no unnecessary lines and a machine no unnecessary parts." In other words, if you bought a new car and looked under the hood, you would be appalled to see unnecessary, functionless parts. Similarly in an essay, all sentences and paragraphs must have an essential function and purpose.

Concision can also be understood through the metaphor of dilution. A word by itself has a sense of power, but when combined with other words, the power of that word is diluted by the presence of the other words, each of which is fighting for the reader's attention. If you want to focus the reader's attention, don't dilute your best words with unnecessary phrases and elaborations.

Establish emphasis

Subordination and coordination allow you to *emphasize* different parts of the sentence, so that the more important phrase is clear. Choosing between subordinate or coordinate clauses alerts you to the hierarchical relationships between information in your sentences and allows you to stress or emphasize certain ideas more than others.

Coordination involves combining clauses in a way that puts them on equal footing, where neither clause is more emphasized than the other. Coordinate clauses are joined with one of the seven coordinating conjunctions – and, but, or, for, so, nor, yet. On the other hand, subordination involves designating one clause to be more important than the other. Subordinate clauses usually begin with although, while, or because.

Use rhythm

If you really want to get fancy with emphasis, you can experiment with periodic and cumulative sentences. Periodic and cumulative sentences are two advanced options for creating a strong sense of rhythm and emphasis in your sentence. The periodic sentence is one in which the main clause is considerably delayed, whereas the cumulative sentence opens quickly with the main clause, and then adds on multiple nonrestrictive clauses after it.

Be straightforward

Beyond any of the above techniques, you can increase the clarity of your writing by practicing a general straightforwardness in the expression of your ideas. Look over your sentences and ask yourself whether they communicate their ideas in the clearest way possible.

You may want to pretend that a twelve-year-old will be reading your text. Will he understand what you're talking about? Remember that while your reader may possess more sophistication than a young child, you don't want to make the reader struggle to follow your ideas. Keep your meaning simple and easy to understand.

To really be clear, you might try talking out your sentences. Imagine yourself saying what you've written to a friend sitting beside you. If you can imagine yourself speaking to your friend with the same sentences you've written, chances are your writing is probably clear and easy to follow. On the other hand, if you can't see yourself saying what you've written to anyone, consider revising it to make it more readable. Go back and revise your sentences to make them friendlier, clearer, more straightforward.

Style

Your style is the fingerprint of your writing and consists of a number of comprising elements. As you edit your essay for style, pay attention to these six areas:

- Personal references
- Diction
- Sentence length
- Sexist pronouns
- Formality
- Emotionalism

Avoid Personal References

Avoid using personal references such as "I" or "In my opinion." It is very easy to say "I feel" or "I think," but this adds little to your essay except a weak argument. If your sentence reads, "I think the Internet is a great source of information," what do the words "I think" add? Rather than supplying a reason for the Internet being a great source of information, the reason given here is "because I think so."

In addition to providing a weak argument, using "I" also takes the focus off the subject and places it on you, the writer, which is sometimes desired in creative writing, but undesirable in an academic essay where the focus is supposed to be on a specific topic. You can usually recast your sentence in a way that omits personal references, but if the sentence just doesn't sound right without "I," then leave it in. It's better to be self-centered than unreadable.

Diction: Choose the right words

Students learning to use a thesaurus often use it excessively and incorrectly in their selection of words. Knowing that all synonyms do not mean the same thing – that each synonym has a subtle nuance of meaning making it distinct from the other words – will help you avoid random substitutions of words that merely seem to look better. Using good diction in your essay involves choosing exactly the right word for the meaning you want. If you're unsure of a word's meaning, look it up in an online dictionary or download a dictionary to your computer.

Vary your sentence length

"Choppiness" is the effect of multiple short sentences in a row giving a sense of breathlessness and childlike simplicity. Contrastingly, the opposite – multiple, successive elongated sentences one after another – gives a sense of never-ending lung power and pompous sophistication. A short sentence can be a good option for the content you're writing, just as a long one can as well. The key is to *mix them up* so that you have some short sentences and some long alternating with each other. This variety will give rhythm to your prose.

Avoid sexist pronouns

Although in the past it was acceptable to use "he" when referring to both men and women, it is no longer acceptable to do so now. Why? Because linguists found that language use actually does have an impact on the way people think and act. If pronouns are always "he," and certain professions are always fire*man*, police*man*, chair*man*, congress*men*, etc, then it is more likely that men – by simple virtue of the privileged masculine pronoun and noun use – will fill those positions, and that women will feel that they do not belong in them. Avoiding sexist pronouns will help you find liberation from these restricting gender roles.

Even if you disagree with the above theory, using "he" only pronouns is a practice that is no longer tolerated in MLA style. You should instead choose to pluralise your subject and use "they" or "their" when referring back to that subject. Or you can choose "he or she," but if you need to write "he or she" more than twice in the sentence, you might give your reader a headache. Try to avoid "s/he" or "he/she" simply because it is unsightly. Really the best solution is pluralisation.

Maintain a level of formality

Just as in daily life, in writing you naturally adjust the level of formality of your writing style to the situation and audience. You may use one level of formality with your teacher, and another level with your best friend. In an academic essay, be sure to maintain a formal voice. One way to adjust your level of formality is by avoiding contractions. However, it is acceptable to use contractions if you desire to.

– *Hyper-formal*: The degree to which private controversial moralities are decriminalised by the federal government depends on the extent of their injurious repercussions on an otherwise benign society.

- *Too informal:* The feds will start putting pervs and whores in the slammer if they feel their smutty actions are mixin' up good men and women.
- *Just right:* Whether private immoralities are outlawed by the government or not depends on the harm they inflict on public society.

Avoid emotionalism

In addition to a formal voice, you should also maintain a cool-headed, objective tone. Tone usually becomes an issue when you are writing about hot topics you feel strongly about – religion, for example, or cultural values. Even when you strongly disagree with an idea, avoid getting "emotional" in your expression. Avoid seeming angry, or condescending, or rude. Keep your calm and remain scholarly, and try to portray yourself as one who is objectively assessing the situation.

- Emotional: We *must* do everything we can to legalise gay marriage. For the sake of equality, the rights of liberty and freedom that our forefathers fought for—it is essential!!! Don't let conservatives take over *your* government and impose their puritanical moral values on everyone. This is only going to lead to dozens of more restrictions that those white-haired conservatives will impose in their cozy congress seats!
- Objective: Keeping gay marriage illegal poses significant questions about the constitutionality

of such laws. The forefathers who wrote the Constitution believed an individual's freedom was vitally important, and that as long as the actions did not cause directly harm to society, the actions should not be decriminalised.

Grammar

As you edit the grammar of your essay, you should particularly focus on the grammar concepts that your teacher has previously marked on your papers. For example, if your teacher has written "run-on" on your previous papers, especially look at the following instruction on run-ons and then look carefully over your essay to make sure you're avoiding them. You should also be familiar with all the rest of the grammar concepts here and be sure that your essay is grammatically correct. If a term below looks unfamiliar, learn it.

Although a grammatically perfect essay won't mean that the essay is also perfect, a teacher is less apt to give you a poor grade if he or she is unable to justify that grade with grammatical errors. In the minds of many old fashioned teachers, perfect grammar equals a perfect essay. When you're done editing for grammar, and you've proofread your essay a dozen times, you're done.

2

Improving Your Letter Writing Skills

Many people are intimidated by writing. Even so, there are times when writing is the best way to communicate, and oftentimes the only way to get your message across.

Letter writing has been used for centuries in communicating across the great oceans, as well as many other facets of communication. Letter writing has a way of bringing people together, but it can also destroy relationships and people. That is why it is so important to make sure that what is written on paper comes across just as the writer meant it. For you see, reading a letter can not only mend a broken heart, but it can bring great joy to the beholder. A letter can offer a complaint, resolve a disagreement, offer an apology, say a thank you, accept an invitation, ask for help, admit blame, and save a soul.

Therefore, it's important to follow the five C's in letter writing, and they are as follows:

1. *Clear*: Try not to beat around the bush when letter writing. Every word should come across as something that is understood. The best way to

test this is to read what you wrote out loud, in a tape recorder, and play it back to yourself.

2. *Concise*: Do not ramble. Try to make your words go straight to the point.
3. *Courteous*: Remember that words can come across a lot harsher on paper. It's best to save arguing to verbal usage, so that you can clear up any misunderstandings.
4. *Correct*: Double check your spelling, grammar, and punctuation. There is nothing worse than trying to read a letter full of mistakes. It makes the clarity of the written word harder to decipher.
5. *Complete*: Make sure that when you bring up a topic, you do not change topics in midstream. Make sure that you finish what you have to say before you go on to another topic.

Personal letters, also known as friendly letters, and social notes normally have five parts.

1. *The Heading*. This includes the address, line by line, with the last line being the date. Skip a line after the heading. The heading is indented to the middle of the page. If using preaddressed stationery, just add the date.
2. *The Greeting*. The greeting always ends with a comma. The greeting may be formal, beginning with the word "dear" and using the person's given name or relationship, or it may be informal if appropriate.

   Formal: Dear Uncle Jim, Dear Mr. Wilkins,

   Informal: Hi Joe, Greetings,

Occasionally very personal greetings may end with an exclamation point for emphasis.

3. *The body.* Also known as the main text. This includes the message you want to write. Normally in a friendly letter, the beginning of paragraphs is indented. If not indented, be sure to skip a space between paragraphs. Skip a line after the greeting and before the close.
4. *The complimentary close.* This short expression is always a few words on a single line. It ends in a comma. It should be indented to the same column as the heading. Skip one to three spaces (two is usual) for the signature line.
5. *The signature line.* Type or print your name. The handwritten signature goes above this line and below the close. The signature line and the handwritten signature are indented to the same column as the close. The signature should be written in blue or black ink. If the letter is quite informal, you may omit the signature line as long as you sign the letter.

WRITING PERSONAL LETTERS

Language Use in a Personal Letter

A personal letter usually has a friendly tone and uses more informal language than a business letter, for example. Formal/informal style is the term given to variation in formality of speech and writing. There is a continuum from the most formal to the most informal.

— Father was fatigued.

— Dad was shattered.

— The old man was stuffed.

The three sentences above have similar meaning; they differ in the degree of formality of style. The first is written in a very formal style; the second and third are increasingly informal. All three examples above are written in standard English. Slang is not the same as vernacular English. It is language in a very informal style of English.

I seen the old man was stuffed.

This sentence is written in a very informal style (slang), and it is in the vernacular. Knowledge of appropriate formal/informal styles of language is an important social skill and one that teachers can help develop. The most formal style will be the most foreign to many students and will require modelling. The most formal style is also the language of academic writing; as students progress through the school, they will need to understand and use this style.

Remember, as letters allow you time to compose your thoughts, you are sending the official a 'hard copy' which can be read several times. Therefore, the nature of letters is such that the content must be very rich and accurate. Letters must be logical and clearly stated. Your argument and your demands must be presented flawlessly and clearly. It is absolutely crucial that your argument be solid, and that you leave no room for interpretations other than yours. Make sure to address every aspect of an argument, and then explain why yours is the preferred one.

Letters should be sent to the individual or governmental body that has the final or most influential say on your issue. It does no good for your cause to send the letter to someone that is not central to the decision making process. Letters should not sound threatening in anyway. An angry official is an irrational official. If you want to accomplish, you must be firm and convincing, but never out right threatening.

Personal letter works covers the following areas and more:

— Letters to family and friends
— Apologies and thank you's
— Dealing with credit problems
— Congratulations and invitations
— Complaints to companies
— Job search
— Letters to doctors and lawyers
— Voicing opinions
— Saying no
— Requests for information
— Letters to builders
— Sympathy and condolences
— and much more.

LETTER TO FAMILY AND FRIENDS

Letters to your family and friends are like conversations. You can write a letter to thank someone, or congratulate them, share family and school news, pass on interesting information, describe what's been happening, or tell funny stories. Maybe you have friends or family who live far away from you. Why not write them a letter to keep in touch? Even if they live close by, a letter is something special that shows you're thinking about them. The great thing about a letter is that you can read it over and over again.

Friendly letters are letters that you write to a friend. They are usually filled with information about you, and ask questions about how your friend is doing. To write a friendly letter, put the date in the upper right hand corner. Begin with a greeting, for example ' Dear Brittany,' Next write the body of the letter. Include all of the information and questions you have for the person you are writing to. Remember to indent each paragraph. When you are finished writing your letter, end with a closing, such as ' Sincerely,' ' Yours truly,' or ' Love,' followed below by your name. When you are finished writing your letter, reread it to see if grammar, punctuation, and spelling is correct, and if what you wrote is clear to the person you are writing to.

WRITING AN APOLOGY LETTER

An apology letter is important to learn how to write for the following reasons: it tells how you feel, it gets a point across, and it helps you practice good writing techniques. Writing an apology letter takes a lot of hard thinking about your's and other's feelings. When you go to apologise to someone you want to make sure that you say/write the right words to satisfy that person's emotions. Sometimes it is hard for us to accept an apology from others; that's why when writing this type of letter, it is very important that you prove to this person that every word you say comes from your heart and is really meant to be accepted.

Another important step is to let the reader know your point in the letter or the reason for deciding to write them this letter. This tells the reader that you are about to make a strong point. In this step you want to make sure that the reader understands what the point is, and/or what it is that you are striving for. The next thing that needs to be acknowledged is not only what the problem is but how to solve it. Let the reader know that you were wrong and that you are sorry. What can you do to make it up to that individual? Then you wait for a strong reply. At this point you should be able to tell whether or not you have made the right decision.

An apology letter can have a positive effect on your writing techniques. Expressing you opinion and creating you own style of writing is the best way to learn good writing techniques. An apology letter does not have any particular rules on how to write them; therefore, the simplest way to understand is to tell how you feel. Just do it!

Guidelines

Here are some tips on how to write your apology with dignity and sincerity:

- Write as soon as possible after the incident. Apologise, but do not go overboard by saying, "I am very, very, very sorry." Keep it simple and to the point. Summarise what you are apologising for, and apologise only for the particular situation or problem. Be brief. Apologise cheerfully and sincerely. Do not express feelings of guilt.
- Explain what you will do to correct the mistake

or situation. Assure the person that this will not happen again.

- Do not put blame on another person and do not blame problems on computer errors or carelessness.
- Thank the person for bringing the problem to your attention if you were unaware of the situation.
- Reread the letter to check your grammar, spelling and tone.

How to Write an Appreciation Letter

Appreciation is a predisposition, an inclination, an openness and readiness of the heart to notice the person who has chosen us, and to sense that our chosen relationship is an awesome thing, not to be taken lightly or for granted. An attitude of appreciation colours our perception of our relationship and everything that happens within it.

Appreciation is a symptom of a successful relationship, a sign that you are completing the unfinished business of past hurts. Rapid healing takes place when you express Appreciation for something that has in the past been a source of anger or hurt for you. It takes raw courage to look your partner in the eye and give them thanks for the lessons you have learned from them. For many couples this face to face stuff is hard, however, believe us in the form of a letter appreciation is just as powerful.

Appreciation letters are so simple that it's a wonder to us that the world isn't overflowing with them. Writing an appreciation letter to your partner is an effective way of showing your love and gratitude. The soft language of appreciation wrapped in a letter which is intimate and special is a powerful way of appreciating your partner.

Try writing a appreciation letter to your partner. We guarantee you they will respond and reciprocate your love!

Use these steps:

- Think of a special name, past or present, that only you call your partner, use this special name in the letter
- Begin the letter with the simple words. "I appreciate you because... "
- Tell your partner the special things you notice about him/her
- Using the following words to start sentences tell your partner how empty your life would be without them. "Without you in my life I would feel.............."
- End the letter by simply saying "I love you"
- Finally, but this is the most important step, place the letter on your partner's pillow or for even more surprise post it to him/her.

Wait and watch what happens! You will be surprised how quickly your partner reciprocates!

WRITE A COMPLAINT LETTER

Effective complaints letters should be: concise, authoritative, factual, constructive, and friendly. Imagine you are receiving a customer's letter of complaint. What type of letter would encourage you to respond positively and helpfully to the complaint? Good complaints letters have these features:

- Concise letters can be understood quickly.
- Authoritative letters - letters that are well written and professionally presented—have more credibility and are taken seriously.
- Factual letters enable the reader to see immediately the relevant details, dates, requirements, etc., and to justify action to resolve the complaint.
- Constructive letters - with positive statements, suggesting positive actions—encourage action and quicker decisions.
- Friendly letters - with a considerate, cooperative and complimentary tone—are prioritised because the reader warms to the writer and wants to help.

These complaints methods are based on cooperation, relationships, constructive problem-solving, and are therefore transferable to phone and face-to-face complaints. A friendly complimentary approach encourages the other person to reciprocate—they'll want to return your faith, build the relationship, and keep you as a loyal customer or user of their products or services. People like helping nice friendly people. People do not find it easy to help nasty people who attack them.

This is perhaps the most important rule of all when complaining. Be kind to people and they will be kind to you. Ask for their help—it's really so simple—and they will want to help you. Contrast a friendly complimentary complaint letter with a complaint letter full of anger and negativity: readers of angry bitter letters are not naturally inclined to want to help—they are more likely to retreat, make excuses, defend, or worse still to respond aggressively or confrontationally. It's human nature.

Also remember that the person reading the letter is just like you—they just want to do a good job, be happy, to get through the day without being upset. What earthly benefit will you get by upsetting them? Be nice to people. Respect their worth and motives. Don't transfer your frustration to them personally—they've not done anything to upset you. They are there to help. The person reading the letter is your best ally—keep them on your side and they will do everything they can to resolve the problem—it's their job.

Try to see things from their point of view. Take the trouble to find out how they work and what the root causes of the problems might be. This friendly approach is essential as well if you cannot resist the urge to pick up the phone and complain. Remember that the person at the other end is only trying to do their job, and that they can only work within the policy that has been issued to them. Don't take it out on them—it's not their fault.

In fact, complaints are best and quickest resolved if you take the view that it's nobody's fault. Attaching blame causes defensiveness—the barriers go up and conflict develops.

Take an objective view—it's happened, for whatever reason; it can't be undone, now let's find out how it can best be resolved. Try to take a cooperative, understanding, objective tone. Not confrontational; instead you and them both looking at the problem from the same side.

If you use phrases like—"I realise that mistakes happen..."; "I'm not blaming anyone...."; "I'm sure this is a rare problem...", your letter (or phone call) will be seen as friendly, non-threatening, and non-confrontational. This relaxes the person at the other end, and makes them more inclined to help you, because you are obviously friendly and reasonable.

The use of humour often works wonders if your letter is to a senior person. Humour dissipates conflict, and immediately attracts attention because it's different. A bit of humour in a complaint letter also creates a friendly, intelligent and cooperative impression.

Senior people dealing with complaints tend to react on a personal level, rather than a procedural level, as with customer services departments. If you brighten someone's day by raising a smile there's a good chance that your letter will be given favourable treatment.

The following information will help you write an effective complaint letter.

- Write the letter as soon as possible after the incident, while it is still fresh in your mind. Type the letter.
- Explain the problem as clearly, briefly, and fairly as possible. In the first and last lines of the letter, clearly state your expectations of the other party.
- Try to confront only one problem at a time. If there are several problems, pick two or three that need immediate attention and briefly list these and how you expect them to be rectified.

— Focus on how the problem can be solved, not on petty details of the problem. Stick to the facts and avoid emotional statements.

— Try to give the letter a polite, positive tone, not a negative tone. Do not use words that express blame. Do not threaten to sue. The objective is to solve the problem and come to some kind of agreement or reimbursement.

— Include all the important information, including dates and times of the occurrence. Include information on how you can be contacted, such as a phone number and address. In case of problems related to merchandise, make copies of documents such as bills and receipts, include the copies with the letter, and keep the originals for your records.

— Conclude your letter with confidence that the matter will be resolved to your satisfaction.

WRITE A CONGRATULATIONS LETTER

Congratulations letters are a form of personal correspondence and are typically sent personally from you to another person.

Although personal in nature, these are routinely sent to co-workers and associates within one's profession. It's not uncommon to send congratulations letters even to competitors. This type of correspondence conveys respect and professionalism that earns the sender a professional reputation and keeps doors open for future dealings, whatever they might be.

Format

Use the friendly format arrangement for congratulations letters:

a. to the right side of the letter header place the return address
b. make two carriage returns
c. directly below the return address, place the date
d. make three carriage returns
e. do not include a reference line
f. begin your letter
g. indent the body paragraphs five spaces each
h. center the closing and signature so that the leftmost character of each are justified to the center of the page if the paper were folded.

Wording

1. Congratulate the reader for their achievement, accomplishment, promotion, etc.
2. In an upbeat tone, tell the reader where you learned of the news.
3. Add a personal note or personal comment of praise in a separate paragraph.
4. Restate your congratulations and wish the reader good luck.

Tone

Keep your tone warm throughout the letter regardless of any personal feelings you may have to the contrary.

Guidelines

Below you will find information that will help you write a wonderful and memorable letter of congratulations.

- Say your best wishes early in the message and again when you close. Make sure you mention the occasion that is being celebrated. Do not add other news or information in the message, with the exception of birthday cards. Express how happy you are for the person and how you learned about the delightful news.
- Avoid going overboard on flattery.
- Be positive and pleasant. If you have an objection about an event, do not include that in your message, or do not write a letter at all.

WRITE AN INVITATION LETTERS

Do you have an engagement, wedding, baby shower, or graduation coming up? Is there a performance, school event, or meeting to which you want to invite people? Any special religious ceremonies like Communion or a Bar Mitzvah? Do you want to invite someone to speak at your meeting or conference? Whatever your event is, the following will help you write an effective invitation.

- State the occasion, date, time, and place. Include addresses and a map if necessary. Mention if refreshments will be served. List any charges that may apply. Include a telephone number for RSVPs. If there is a dress code, state the preferred dress in the lower left-hand corner of the card.

- If you need a response, include a self-addressed, stamped reply card or envelope with your invitation.
- Express that you are looking forward to seeing the person.
- Do not use abbreviations and do not use contractions (don't; we'll) except for name titles, such as Mr., Mrs., etc.
- If dinner will be served, state two separate times: the time people can start arriving and the time dinner will be served.
- If you do not want gifts, briefly state that gifts are not wanted or needed. Explain that their presence is the only gift you need.
- Make sure you send your invitations out with ample advance notice.
- If you have guests coming from out of town or from other countries, you may want to send out your invitation several months in advance (especially if your event takes place around a holiday.) This will allow your guests adequate time to make preparations, reservations, save money, etc.
- For smaller, less formal events that include local guests or guests from nearby areas, you may only need to provide a few weeks notice.
- If you are inviting someone to speak at a conference, your invitation should include the following information:
  - Name of the conference and the sponsoring organisation;

  - Date, time, place of the conference and speech;
  - Type of audience;
  - The type of speech, topic, and how long the speech should be;
- Any accommodations that will be made, including lodging, meals, and transportation;
- The name of the contact person along with phone numbers and addresses where the person can be contacted; and
- Finally, articulate your pleasure of having the person speak at the meeting or conference.

WRITE A CONDOLENCE LETTER

One of the most meaningful acts of kindness you can do for a mourner is to write a letter of condolence. The words of sympathy and memory are comforting to the bereaved. More importantly, mourners are very appreciative that you took the time to sit and compose a personal message to them or share a memory of the deceased. Mourners often save these letters for years.

Yet, the apparently simple act of writing a condolence letter is a lost art. Actually, letter-writing itself is a skill in danger of extinction, given the ease of calling on the phone. Of course, you can purchase commercially available condolence cards and add your own brief message, but a well-crafted, personal letter of condolence is a wonderful gift to a mourner.

A good condolence letter has two goals: to offer tribute to the deceased and to be a source of comfort to the survivors. The best letters are like conversations on paper-free-flowing as if you were talking during a visit. Most often, they are written to the bereaved person to whom you feel closest although it could be a general letter to the family. It should be written and sent promptly, generally within two weeks after the death. Use any standard stationery and write it by hand. Some etiquette experts recommend brevity, although if you have particular stories you wish to tell about the deceased, the letter may be lengthy.

Here are some specific guidelines for writing a good condolence letter.

— *Acknowledge the loss and name of the deceased.* This sets the purpose and tone of the letter. Let the bereaved know how you learned of the death and how you felt upon hearing the news. Using the name of the deceased is a tribute that comforts most mourners.

— *Express your sympathy.* Let the bereaved know your sadness. Use words of sympathy that share your own sorrow. This will remind the bereaved they are not alone in their suffering.

— *Note special qualities of the deceased.* Acknowledge those characteristics that you cherished most about the person who has died. These might be qualities of personality (leadership, sensitivity), or attributes (funny, good at sports), or ways the person related to the world (religious, devoted to community welfare). You might write of the special relationship you noted between the deceased and the bereaved.

— *Recall a memory about the deceased.* Tell a brief story or anecdote that features the deceased. Try to capture what it was about the person in the story that you admired, appreciated or respected. Talk about how the deceased touched your life. Use humour-the funny stories are often the most appreciated by the bereaved.

— *Remind the bereaved of their personal strengths.* Bereavement often brings with it self-doubt and anxiety about one's own personal worth. By reminding the bereaved of the qualities they possess that will help them through this period, you reinforce their ability to cope. Among these qualities might be patience, optimism, religious belief, resilience, competence, and trust. If you can recall something the deceased used to say about the mourner in this regard, you will really be giving your friend a gift.

— *Offer help, but be specific.* "If there is anything I can do, please call" actually puts a burden on those in grief who may be totally at a loss about what needs to be done. A definite offer to help with shopping, the kids, volunteer work, or whatever is more appreciated. Or offer to contact the mourner after the initial shiva period when the commotion has subsided. Then, do it-don't make an offer you can't fulfil.

— *End with a word of phrase or sympathy.* Somehow, "sincerely," "love," or "fondly," don't quite make it. Try one of these:

  — "You are in my thoughts and prayers."

  — "Our love is with you always."

  — "We share in your grief and send you our love."

– "My affectionate respects to you and yours."

Of course, the traditional greeting to mourners is also an excellent close:

– "May God comfort you among the other mourners of Zion and Jerusalem."

WRITING BUSINESS LETTERS

A good business letter is brief, straightforward, and polite. If possible, it should be limited to one single-spaced typewritten page. Because it is so brief, a business letter is often judged on small, but important, things: format, grammar, punctuation, openings and closings. A business letter is not the place to try out fancy fonts or experimental writing styles.

There are two main styles of business letters:

– *Full block style*: Align all elements on the left margin.

– *Modified block style*: Down the middle of the page, align the return address, date, closing, signature, and typed name; align other elements on the left page margin.

Below are the elements of a standard business letter and their functions:

– *Return Address*: Your address (or the address of the company you represent). If you are using preprinted stationary, there is no need to retype the information.

– *Date:* Leave two blank lines after the return address. Always spell out the month and include the day, a comma, and the year.

- *Inside Address*: Leave two blank lines after the date. Then type the address of the person or company to whom you are writing.
- *Salutation*: Type Dear, followed by the person's name. End the line with a colon. If you don't know the name of the person, use a title instead.
- *Body*: Align your message on the left margin. Skip a line before starting a new paragraph, but do not indent the paragraph's first line. Make sure that each paragraph is clear and concise.
- *Closing*: Leave two lines of space after your last body paragraph, then use a conventional closing, followed by a comma.
- *Signature*: Your signature should appear below your closing. Unless you have established a personal relationship with the person you are writing, use both your first and last name.
- *Name and Position*: Four lines after the closing, type your full name. Do not include a title (Mr. or Mrs.). If you are writing on behalf of an organisation, type your title on the next line.
- *Abbreviations at the end of a letter*: If you send a copy of a letter to someone other than the person addressed, use cc: and the person's name. Use Enc. or Enclosure if you enclose something with the letter. If someone else types it, put the writer's initials in capitals, then a slash and the typist's initials in lowercase:

  MT/fjr. Just one abbreviation should appear on a line.

You will write business letters to inform readers of specific information. However, you might also write a business letter to persuade others to take action or to propose your ideas. Business letters even function as advertisements at times. Consider the letters long-distance phone companies send to those not signed up for their services or the cover letter to your resume. Both of these serve to promote or advertise. Business letters can be challenging to write, because you have to consider how to keep your readers' attention. This is particularly the case if your readers receive large amounts of mail and have little time to read.

Writing business letters is like any other document: First you must analyse your audience and determine your purpose. Then you gather information, create an outline, write a draft, and revise it. The key to writing business letters is to get to the point as quickly as possible and to present your information clearly.

The basics of good business letter writing are easy to learn. The following guide provides the phrases that are usually found in any standard business letter. These phrases are used as a kind of frame and introduction to the content of business letters.

Start

Dear Personnel Director, Dear Sir or Madam (use if you don't know who you are writing to) Dear Mr, Mrs, Miss or Ms (use if you know who you are writing to, and have a formal relationship with. Use Ms for women unless asked to use Mrs or Miss) Dear Frank (use if the person is a close business contact or friend).

Reference

- With reference to your advertisement in the *Times,*
- your letter of 23 rd March,
- your phone call today,
- Thank you for your letter of March 5 th.

Reason for Writing

- I am writing to enquire about
- apologise for confirm

Requesting

- Could you possibly?
- I would be grateful if you could

Agreeing to Requests

- I would be delighted to

Giving Bad News

- Unfortunately
- I am afraid that

Enclosing Documents

- I am enclosing
- Please find enclosed
- Enclosed you will find

Closing Remarks

- Thank you for your help

- Please contact us again if we can help in any way.
- there are any problems.
- you have any questions.

Reference to Future Contact

- I look forward to...
- hearing from you soon.
- meeting you next Tuesday.
- seeing you next Thursday.

Finish

- Yours faithfully, (If you don't know the name of the person you're writing to)
- Yours sincerely, (If you know the name of the person you're writing to)
- Best wishes,
- Best regards, (If the person is a close business contact or friend)

COVER LETTERS

If you think you don't need to put much effort into writing cover letters -- or don't need to send them at all because nobody reads them -- think again. True, many recruiters, headhunters and department heads don't have time to read both the letter and resume, so they skip right to the resume. Others are so tired of boring letters saying the same old thing that they simply don't bother to read them. As a result, some job-search coaches will tell you, "Oh, just write a few sentences and don't fuss over the letter too much. It won't get read anyway."

Well, for every person who says the cover letter is not important, you'll find another who says it is. Many prospective employers view the cover letter as a way of getting their first impression of you. The cover letter reveals:

— How well you communicate.

— What your experience and qualifications are -- briefly.

— Your level of professionalism.

— Clues to your personality.

— How detail oriented you are (i.e., are there typos or other errors?).

To make the best first impression, you need to know exactly what a cover letter is and to put some thought into it before you start writing. You also need to understand what to include -- and not to include -- and to be aware of some cardinal rules of cover letter writing.

A cover letter is an introduction, a sales pitch and a proposal for further action all in one. It gives the reader a taste of what's to come—not by simply summarising the resume, but by highlighting the aspects of your background that will be most relevant to the reader. A cover letter also demonstrates that you can organise your thoughts and express yourself clearly and appropriately; in other words, it reflects your communication skills and, to some extent, your personality.

Cover letters are typically one-page documents. Like lots of things in life, they have a beginning, middle and end: usually an introduction saying who you are and why you're writing, followed by a sales pitch of what you have to offer and then a closing in which you propose steps for further action. These three components often amount to three or four paragraphs, but there are no hard and fast rules about exactly how you break up the information.

Thinking About Before Writing

If you find yourself struck by writer's block at about the "Dear Mr. or Ms. So-and-So" point, then you probably need to take a step back and put some more thought into your cover letter before diving into it. Asking yourself the following five questions will help you build a foundation for your letter and will make the actual writing go much more smoothly.

- What does the prospective employer need? Which skills, knowledge and experience would be an asset in the job you are targeting?
- What are your objectives? Are you applying for a specific job, trying to get an interview or simply hoping to get someone to spend 10 or 15 minutes on the phone with you discussing opportunities in general at that organisation?
- What are three to five qualities that you would bring to this employer or this job? If you're responding to a job listing or classified, then those qualities should obviously be the job requirements mentioned in the ad. If you're not applying for a specific job opening, then think of which skills, knowledge and experience would typically be valued.
- How can you match your experience to the job? What are at least two specific accomplishments

you can mention that give credence to the qualities you identified in question number 3?

- Why do you want to work for this particular organisation or person? What do you know about the company? What is it about its products or services, philosophy, mission, organisational culture, goals and needs that relates to your own background, values and objectives?
- When you've addressed these five issues, you're ready to put fingers to keyboard and start hammering out that letter.

Structure

If you're bewildered by how you're actually going to write a cover letter, it can help to break the letter down into its various parts and concentrate on just one section at a time. Here's what goes into each of the four main sections of a cover letter:

Opening

This is where you tell employers who you are, why you're writing and how you heard about the organisation or the specific opening. The "who you are" part is a brief introduction of yourself with a phrase like: "I am a senior at XYZ University graduating in May with a major in biology." Just mention the basic facts about you and your situation, choosing the ones that will be most relevant to the employer.

The "why you're writing" part is where you mention which position you are applying for, or what your job objective is if no specific opening has been advertised. Then be sure to say how you heard about the organisation or the job. You might say, for example, "I saw your listing for a textile designer at the Career Development Office of the Rhode Island School of Design." Or, "I read about the expansion of your East Coast operations in the New York Times and am interested in discussing entry-level opportunities you might have available."

Sales pitch

In this section, it's best to get right to the point. The objective of this part of the letter is to list, either in paragraph form or as an actual list of bullet points, the reasons why the reader should see you as a viable candidate. It's best to start with a statement that provides an overview of your qualifications, then go into them more specifically, using the examples you identified before you started writing. A typical opening statement might sound something like: "As a political science major and former Congressional intern, I offer the following skills and accomplishments."

Flattery

This is the "why them" section of your letter. It's where you flatter the reader a bit by commenting on something positive about the organisation and saying why you would want to work there. You might mention the organisation's reputation, sales record, size, corporate culture, management philosophy or anything else managers take pride in. Prospective employers like to know that you have chosen them for a reason and that they're not just one of hundreds of companies you're writing to as part of a mass mailing.

Request for further action

Some people think of this final section of a cover letter as the closing, but it's much more than that. The closing paragraph isn't just about thanking the reader for taking the time to read your letter or for considering you as a candidate for a job. It's also about where to go from here, about opening the door to further contact. It's where you suggest how to proceed, usually by saying that you will call or email the reader to follow up and see if a meeting can be arranged. The important thing is to end the letter in an assertive, but courteous, way by taking the initiative to follow up.

Once you've getting these four sections of the letter completed in terms of content, go back and smooth out any rough edges of your writing and check for typos, misspellings and grammatical errors. Then you're ready for "Sincerely" or "Best Regards" and your signature, and you're off and running on the road to a great job.

Rules

— Tailor your letter as much as possible to the target reader and industry.

— Talk more about what you can do for the prospective employer than about what they can do for you.

— Convey focused career goals. Even if you'd be willing to take any job they'd offer you, don't say so.

— Don't say anything negative about your employment situation or your life in general.

- Cut to the chase -- don't ramble.
- Don't make empty claims that aren't backed up with examples.
- Don't write more than one page unless the prospective employer has asked for a detailed or extended cover letter.
- Check, recheck and triple check your letter for typos and other errors.
- Get other people's opinions of your letter before you send it.
- Keep easily accessible copies of all letters you mail, fax or email along with a log of when letters were sent so that you can follow up on them.

Guidelines

- Do your homework! Modify your letter to fit the company and their needs. Include any information appropriate to the job you are applying for.
- Show concern, interest, and pride for your profession and your skills.
- State briefly what is enclosed. If there are several items, list them. Keep the letter simple and to the point. Tell the truth. Don't try to be overly friendly, but don't be too remote either.
- Include your telephone number or numbers where you can be contacted. When writing the letter, address the person you are sending it to, not to a title.

— Indicate any response you are expecting from the company. Ask for the next step, such as an interview or some other meeting.

— Cover letters that are sent to job search firms or employment agencies should include your current or expected salary if requested and note if you are willing to relocate.

— Add relay information if you are deaf/ hard-of-hearing and your prospective employer is hearing. Be sure to briefly explain how to use the relay service.

WRITING A RESUME

Writing a resume is crucial in the work force because it is essential to obtaining a job, it is your personal advertisement to an employer, and it is the most accepted form of communication between you and an employer.

Essential for Jobs

A resume is a crucial link to obtaining a job in the work force. One must have an effective resume to arouse interest in the employer and put all thoughts of other applicants aside. Without a resume, one might not get an interview or a job. The resume is the key to the door of the work force; and with that key, you open the door to many opportunities

Personal Advertisement

A resume is a personal advertisement of yourself and why you are the best candidate for the job. One must "advertise" them self as an effective employee: one who has the best qualifications for the particular position that is being applied for. Resumes should contain any information that will enable you to obtain the job. If you are applying for a clerical position, you might want to put things on your resume that would apply to that position: the ability to type 50 words per minute, any computer and data entry courses, able to utilise word processing programmes, etc. Your resume should fit your personal abilities and no one else.

Communication Between the Employer and You

The resume you send out must be exciting and attractive to the eye since it is the only and most accepted form of communication between you and an employer. The resume must contain six essential elements:

1. *Full name, address and phone number (No abbreviations)*
2. *An Objective*: Seeking a ____ position in an organisation where _____, _____ and ____skills will be needed and utilised.
3. *A Summary:* The summary is your chance to tell the employer of all the activities that you are involved in. This is where you should list accomplishments. If you have a long list of awards, place them in a category of their own. You should also list any skills on the resume that would apply to the job that you are applying for.
4. *A List of Job Experiences:* If you have never had a job before, list volunteer work or work that would help you in the job that you want to get. The list should begin from the present and work

its way to the very first job you had as the last entry.

5. *Education:* This an important part of a resume. This portion contains all of your educational background starting from with college, vocational school and lastly, high school.
6. *References*: References will be furnished upon request. Make sure that when an employer asks you for a reference sheet that you have one on hand and ready for use.

Guidelines

- Include your name, address and daytime phone number. Include any relay information if needed.
- Include your job objective. The objective should explain what job you are applying for. It could also include how that position fits into your personal career goals.
- Describe your work experience, education, honors/awards and skills.
- You do not need to include every single job you have ever had. You should focus on your education and experiences that are related to the position for which you are applying.
- However, try to avoid any large time breaks between jobs listed on your resume. The employer may think you were unemployed during that time.
- Prepare a list of references, if requested, on a separate page. This list should include two to three names, job titles, addresses and phone

numbers of bosses, professors, etc. who will confirm that you have good work ethic.

— Write a cover letter on a separate page. The cover letter should be personalised for each job you are applying for.

— Tell the truth; do not exaggerate or tell half-truths. Show that you are confident and well-educated.

— Your resume should be typed. Your layout and word choice should be clear and simple. Double-check your resume before turning it in.

— Avoid attempts at humour and irrelevant information. Avoid unnecessary personal information about your age, weight, finances, and marital status.

— Do not mention salary on your resume.

— Avoid using adjectives and adverbs. Use powerful or unusual nouns and verbs instead. Don't make the resume too wordy. Try to use as few words as possible and still make it effective. Most resumes shouldn't be more than one page, unless you are someone who has several years of experience (10+ years) in your field.

USEFUL PHRASES FOR LETTER WRITING

Personal and Social Correspondence

Openings

The standard opening for personal correspondence is Dear but variations include:

My dear ...

My dearest ...

Darling ...

Useful phrases

- Thank you for your letter [inviting, offering, confirming]
- I am delighted to announce that
- I am very grateful to you for [letting me know, offering, writing]
- I was delighted to hear that
- It was so kind of you to [write, invite, send]
- I am sorry to inform you that
- Many thanks for [sending, inviting, enclosing]
- I was so sorry to hear that
- I am writing to tell you that

Closures

For acquaintances and formal situations:

- Best wishes
- With best wishes
- Kindest regards

Affectionate variations for close friends and family:

All my love	See you soon
All the best	Once again many thanks
Love	I look forward to seeing you soon
Lots of love	With love and best wishes
Much love	With love to you all

With love	Do give my kindest regards to ...
Love from us both	

Letters about Employment

Openings

The standard opening for formal correspondence is Dear.

Dear Sir	Dear Mr
Dear Madam	Dear Mrs
Dear Sir or Madam	
Dear Ms	Dear Sirs

Useful phrases

- I am writing in response to your advertisement in [publication]
- Thank you for your letter of [date] offering me the post of
- I am writing to apply for the post of
- I am delighted to accept the position of [job title]
- I should be pleased to attend an interview
- I look forward to starting work with you

Closures

- Thank you for considering this application
- I should be pleased to attend an interview
- Please do not hesitate to contact me on the above number if you should require further information

- I look forward to hearing from you
- If you know the name of the person use: Yours sincerely
- If you don't know the name of the person use: Yours faithfully.

Business Letters

Openings

The standard opening for formal correspondence is Dear

Dear Sir	Dear Mr
Dear Madam	Dear Mrs
Dear Sir or Madam	Dear Ms
Dear Sirs	

Useful phrases

- Thank you for your letter of [date] concerning
- I apologise for the delay in replying
- Thank you for sending me a [catalogue, quotation]
- As stated in your letter/fax of [date]
- Thank you for your enquiry of [date]
- I wish to draw your attention to the
- I refer to your letter of [date] concerning
- I wish to inform you that
- Further to our telephone conversation of [date]
- I am writing to inform you that
- I am writing to confirm our telephone conversation of [date]

- I am writing to express my dissatisfaction with
- I would be grateful if you could forward me a [price list, catalogue]
- Please note that
- I am contacting you regarding
- Please find enclosed
- I am writing to complain

Closures

- I look forward to hearing from you
- I trust that you will give this matter your urgent attention
- I look forward to hearing your response
- I hope you can settle this matter to my satisfaction
- I would be most grateful if you would look into this matter as soon as possible
- Please do not hesitate to contact me should you require further information
- Please let me know as soon as possible what action you propose to take
- Please contact me if you require further details

3

Developing Sentence Making Skills

The sentence that raises a subject and says something about it is an independent sentence. It makes a statement that has sense and only one sense. Such a statement has only three structural models, or 'basic-sentence' types. They are the verb sentence, the copula sentence and the copular-verb sentence. The independent sentence is the typical written sentence. It is the one we depend on when we write an essay, an article for a periodical, a thesis – in short, when we write in any genre that does not require us to represent casual-speech structures.

SUBJECT AND PREDICATE

The sentence raises a subject and says something about it. To put it another, more formal, way: The sentence predicates something of the subject. This is all that Traditional Grammar means when it declares that the sentence consists of a subject and a predicate.

Indispensable Basic Sentence

No sequence of words is a sentence if it fails to make one unambiguous sense. No sequence of words makes one unambiguous sense unless it is a basic sentence or it contains one. Stripped of its basic sentence, this sequence makes no sense:

> *very best a dog called Caesar contemporary street.*

It becomes sensible only when a basic sentence holds it together:

> *My very best friend, a dog called Caesar, does not respect contemporary street sculpture.*

Writers must become so familiar with the three models of the basic sentence that one 'jumps out' at them from every sentence they read. Such a level of familiarity will ensure that the sentences they write will never fail to meet the first and most important criterion of valid sentence-construction: the unmistakable presence of a basic sentence. It will ensure also that they are able to punctuate the longer sentences they write.

VERB MODEL OF BASIC SENTENCE

In the verb model of the basic sentence there always is a specific relationship between the subject and object in a sentence. In every instance of a verb basic sentence the subject and object relate in one the following ways:

Subject Acts Upon the Object

In this sentence:

> *Nationalism alarms minorities,*

the subject 'nationalism' perpetrates an act, denoted by the verb 'alarms', upon the object 'minorities'. Traditional Grammar says of sentences in which the subject acts upon the object that they are active voice sentences.

subject	predicate	
	verb	*object*
Nationalism	alarms	minorities.
The man	opened	the gate.

Object Acts Upon the Subject

In this sentence:

A will to live is developed by the endangered

the object 'the endangered' acts upon the subject 'a will to live'. The verb 'develop' denotes this act. Traditional Grammar says of sentences in which the object acts upon the subject that they are sentences cast in the passive voice mode. As all verb sentences, this one has an active voice too, as the grid shows:

subject	predicate	
	verb	*object*
A will to live	is developed	by the endangered (noun phrase)
The endangered	develop (noun phrase)	a will to live.

'Infinitive' complications and the complemented verb

There are infinitives that consist of more than 'to' and one word: 'To set' is one infinitive, 'to set free' quite another. Their meanings are different, just like the meanings of 'to give' and 'to give up' are different. They are the cause of structures such as 'He set me free', in which the object 'me' comes between the parts of the infinitive. These structures are otherwise ordinary active-voice verb sentences that typically also have a passive voice: 'I was set free by him'. This situation is less obvious in the infinite that seems to have a 'to make (someone) do' structure. We meet this structure regularly in statements such as:

> *He made me clean the house/wash dishes/laugh (active voice).*

There is no doubt that this, too, is a sentence in which the subject acts upon the object (active voice), or the object acts upon the subject (passive voice):

> *I was made to clean the house/wash dishes/laugh by him (passive voice).*

So this is certainly a verb sentence. The curious thing is that in the passive voice sentence the verb changes to the phrase 'was made to clean'. This reveals that the real object in this sentence is 'the house', not 'me'. However, it is indisputable that the subject 'he' acts upon the object 'me'.

subject		predicate	
	verb	*object*	*compliment*
He	made	me (direct)	clean the house.
I	was made to clean	the house (indirect) by him (direct).	

Subject and Object Devolves upon a Third Party

As subject and object perpetrate an act upon one another, a third party is affected by the action. So in 'He read me the Riot Act' the subject 'he' perpetrated an act upon the object 'Riot Act': he read it. The 'riot' act is therefore the direct object of the subject's activity that is denoted by the verb 'read'. This subject acts also upon 'me'. So 'me' is also an object. But it is not the direct object that the subject acts upon: it is the indirect object of the subject's activity 'read':

subject		predicate
	verb	*object*
He	read	me (indirect) the Riot Act (direct).
The minister		read the Riot Act (direct) to the marchers (indirect).

Activity between Subject and Object

In this sentence:

He called them liars,

the subject 'he' acts upon the object 'them'. To this extent, this sentence is of the type outlined in '1'. It differs from it markedly, however, in that the noun 'liars' is embedded into the '1' sort of structure, 'he called them', to name the content of the activity 'called'. That noun is not an object at all. It is therefore in no way possible to call it an 'indirect object'. Other sentences of the same structure are:

The boy taught his grandmother Mathematics

The boy taught his grandmother to suck eggs.

The subject 'the boy' perpetrated the act denoted by the verb 'taught' on the object 'his grandmother'. The content of the subject's act is named by the noun 'Mathematics' in the first sentence, and by the infinitive-noun phrase 'to suck eggs' in the second.

subject		predicate	
	verb	*object*	*activity-naming noun complement*
He	called	them	liars.
The boy	taught	his grandmother	Mathematics.
The boy	taught	his grandmother	to suck eggs.

Subject Acts Upon Object

In this sentences:

The film had me laughing

the subject 'the film' acted upon the object 'me' to put it into a laughing state. The meaning here can be paraphrased as 'he had me in a laughing state'. 'In a laughing state' names the existential state of the object 'me'. The actual sentence, however, has truncated the noun phrase to 'laughing'. The truncation nevertheless functions as a noun in this sentence, as the paraphrasing indicates that it must. It is a noun embedded into the basic sentence 'he had me'. In another sentence:

He sat me in the front row

an embedded noun phrase with the same function, 'in the front row', is kept in entirety to name the whereabouts of the object 'me'. It, too, is embedded into the verb basic sentence.

Object is the Experiencer of the Act

In this sentence:

John interests Mary

the subject 'John' certainly perpetrates an act upon the object 'Mary'. But only the object 'Mary' experiences the effect of that act. The subject 'John' may not even be aware that he has perpetrated that act. This situation exits because there are verbs that are inherently object-experiencer verbs. These are: annoy, irritate, amaze, provoke, impress, interest. Some of their synonyms might also prove to be object-experiencer verbs in some constructions.

'Subject + Verb' Sentence as the Basic Sentence

Where the basic sentence is a 'verb + subject' sentence nothing is predicated of the subject other than that the subject does, has done or will do something:

Mary teaches.

Mary has taught.

The Prime Minister will resign.

All that can happen in the 'verb + subject' sentence is that certain indicators describe the subject's act. Those indicators are adverbs. They describe:

— when (time) the subject perpetrated an act:

She arrived early;

— how (manner) the subject perpetrated an act:

The girl answered slowly,

The girl came begging;

— the intensity (degree) of the subject's act:

We could hardly see.

It has been claimed, thanks to the 'subject + predicate' sentence, that describing sentence structure is a sham. The claimants argued that Traditional Grammar holds that 'Mother is cooking' and 'Dinner is cooking' are sentences of the same syntactic structure. If Traditional Grammar's system of analysis were constrained to do that, it would indeed be a sham. But it is not so constrained.

The sentence 'Mother is cooking' (Mother is doing the cooking) is a 'verb + subject' sentence.

'Dinner is cooking' is a copula sentence in which the predicate adjective 'cooking' describes the subject 'dinner' ('the cooking dinner').

COPULA MODEL OF BASIC SENTENCE

The copula model of the basic sentence makes a statement in which the copula assigns the subject either a description or a definition or a location (geographical or existential) or an occupier.

In behaving thus, the copula basic sentence is completely different from the verb basic sentence. It has to be different because there is no relationship of subject and object in it. Indeed, the copula sentence does not have an object. It has instead a complement.

Copular Assigns a Description to the Subject

In the sentences that follow, the copular has the complement describe the subject. A description that occurs in this way is called a predicate adjective if it is achieved by a single word, and predicate-adjective phrase if it is achieved by a sequence of words. In the sentence:

John was ill/annoying/pleased

the copula assigns the description 'ill' (or 'annoying' or 'pleased') to the subject 'John'. In the next sentence:

Walking to school might have been as bad as you say

the copula 'might have been' assigns the description 'as bad as you say' to the subject 'walking to school'.

Copula Assigns a Definition to the Subject

This activity of the copula has the complement define the subject. In:

Practice is what you need

the copula 'is' defines the subject 'practice' in terms of the noun phrase 'what you need'. In the next sentence:

To know that you are well has always been all I asked

the copula phrase 'has always been' has the complement 'all I have ever asked' define the subject 'To know that you are well'.

Copula Assigns a Place in Space to the Subject

In this role the copula has the complement name the location of the subject. In so doing it names the place that, geographically speaking, the subject occupies (or did or will occupy). The complement in such sentences names a geographic location (which is necessarily a place). It is therefore a locative noun phrase when it names a place ('John was in London/ at the party'), and a locative pronoun when it refers to a place ('John was here/there').

Copula Assigns a Place in Existential Space to the Subject

In this role the copula has the complement tell us where the subject is on a spiritual, ethical, moral, professional, etc. plane. In:

He is beyond recall

the subject 'he' is located by the copula 'is' in some spiritual (or ethical or moral) space that is named by the noun phrase 'beyond recall'. In the sentence:

They were in mourning

the subject 'they' is located by the copula 'were' in the spiritual space named by the noun phrase 'in mourning'. In the sentence:

She had been on duty.

the subject 'she' is located by the copula phrase 'had been' in her professional space, named by the noun phrase 'on duty'.

Copula Effects the Occupation

When the copula sentence does not name a subject but erects a token one instead ('It', 'That', 'What') the erection is a vacant one yet to be filled with the naming capacity (a noun or noun phrase) of the complement. The copula directs that this filling, or occupying, take place. Thus in the sentence:

It is true that he is happy.

the copula 'is' directs the noun phrase 'that he is happy' to occupy the vacant subject 'It'. This occupation is evident in that the noun phrase can sensibly take the place of the subject:

It is true that he is happy.

That he is happy is true.

Subjects 'It' and 'That' are Not Always Vacant Subjects

The vacant subject should not be confused with 'It' subjects that are not vacant. In this sentence 'It' represents the subject raised in an earlier sentence:

This machine is in good order. It was fixed yesterday.

In this sentence 'That' represents the sense 'the person you saw who was not me':

'I am sure I saw you there.'

'No. That was my sister.'

No adverb in a copula sentence

The important characteristic of the copula sentence is that it does not contain an adverb. This is no more than logical, for adverbs modify verbs, and the copula sentence does not contain a verb, for the simple reason that it is a copula (not a 'verb') sentence. Now, it might seem that this copula sentence:

He is really ill

contains the adverb 'really'. But it does not, for 'really' modifies the predicate adjective 'ill'. Modifying an adjective, a word cannot be said to be functioning as an adverb. Rather, 'really' is itself an adjective. It has exactly the same function as 'very', or any other degree/intensity-setting qualifier of an adjective: He is very/dangerously/etc. ill. (For some reason that is not at all easy to identify, Traditional Grammar tends to call these qualifiers 'adverbs of degree'. We suggest that 'adjectives of degree' is by far the more perspicacious term.)

Critics of the observation that there is no adverb in a copula sentence have proposed that sentences such as:

It is really John / It really is John

refute that observation. These critics rely on the erroneous assumption that 'really' is by nature an adverb. Well, it is not, as we noted in the sentence 'He is really ill'. Just as in that sentence 'really' pertains to the predicate adjective 'ill', so in the above sentences 'really' pertains to the noun 'John'. And, pertaining to a noun, it is necessarily an adjective. 'Is' in these sentences effects the occupation by the complement 'really John' of the two vacant subjects 'It'.

COPULAR-VERB MODEL OF BASIC SENTENCE

The copular verb looks like a verb. However, like the copula, it does not have an object. It has a complement. Characteristically, the complement determines something about the activity denoted by the copular verb:

Complement Locates the Place of the Subject's Act

In the sentence:

He rested in bed

there is no object: Rather, the subject's act 'rested' is located by the by the noun-phrase complement 'in bed'. Simply, 'in bed' names the place where the subject 'he' performed the act denoted by the copular verb 'rested'. Some other place-namer functions of the complement are illuminated on this grid:

Existential Character of Subject's Act

Whether the existential character of the subject's act is named prosaically:

The girl left in a hurry

or metaphorically:

The girl left in high dudgeo

it is a fact that the complement specifies the character of the subject's act by naming its identity.

The identity of 'left' in the foregoing sentences is the 'in a hurray' or 'in high dudgeon' version of the act denoted by 'left'. Other identity-namers of the act denoted by 'left' might be 'in a leisurely manner', 'without regret', etc. These identity-namers of the subject's act are nouns for the simple reason that they name.

When the copular verb itself identifies its own character, as in this sentence:

The pair raved about the trip

its orientation (or 'direction' or 'bent') is further identified by a noun-phrase complement. The same reasoning informs the analysis of the sentence 'He talked of morality'. The subject's act, denoted by the copular-verb 'talked', is said to have an 'of morality' bent, just as the subject's act, denoted by the copular-verb 'raved', is said to have an 'about the trip' bent. In exactly the same way, the complement identifies the bent of the subject's act with an -ing ending noun:

I went fishing. / We go dancing.

Without the direction-naming service of the nouns 'fishing' and 'dancing', the copular verbs 'went' and 'go' would not be capable of denoting an activity.

Context of the Subject's Act

In this sentences:

The comment was uttered in jest/on the spur of the moment

there is no activity at all. There is instead a locating of the subject 'the comment' in an 'uttered-in-jest' and an uttered-on-the-spur-of-the-moment context. It is clear in these sentences that the point made about the subject 'the comment' is not that it perpetrated an act. The point is that the act was perpetrated in a particular context.

Content of the Subject's Act

In the sentence:

The bushman predicted that there will be a storm

the noun-phrase 'that there will be a storm' names the content of the act 'predicted' of the subject 'the bushman'. It was an act of storm-prediction. The other sentences on the grid also have compound-noun meaning templates like 'storm-prediction: 'war-prophecy', 'revenge-threat', 'nonsense-talk'.

Purpose of the Subject's Act

Sentences like:

I live to please you

and

They shouted to warn him

are all too easy to mistake for verb sentences in which 'live to please' is the verb phrase, 'I' the subject and 'you' the object. That the subject does not act upon the object is made clear in their passive-voice cast:

To please you is why I live

To warn him is why they shouted.

Nothing attests more clearly than this cast that 'to please you' and 'to warn him' are noun phrases. And the 'why' component of both sentences attests to the purpose-naming role of the noun phrases.

Purpose-naming roles are performed also by 'for'-headed noun phrases.

Subject and Complement Depict their Genitive Relationship

In the sentence:

The soldiers had orders

there is no activity. There is only the depiction of a genitive relationship between the subject 'the soldiers' and the noun complement 'orders'. The relationship depicted here has the meaning-template 'soldiers' orders'. In the other sentence on the grid, the meaning template is 'the child's doll'.

Complement Joins Copular Verb to Describe the Subject

In both these sentences:

The chicken was fried crisp

He waxed lyrical/indignant

there are the predicate-adjective complements 'crisp', 'lyrical' and 'indignant'. Being predicate adjectives, they necessarily describe the noun subject 'the chicken' and pronoun subject 'he'. In neither sentence is the subject described by the predicate adjective alone. That is, the subject 'the chicken' is not described merely as 'crisp'; it is described as 'crisp fried'. And the subject 'he' is not described only as 'lyrical'; it is described as 'waxed-lyrical' and 'waxed indignant'. In this sense, the copular verb is part of the description that a predicate-adjective complement makes of the subject.

INDEPENDENT SENTENCE STYLES

There are only four styles of sentences that make

statements. These styles are infinitely accommodating and flexible. They do not limit our self-expression any more than does the fact that all our reasoning procedures are either inductive or deductive. It is a writer's way of thinking about what he wants to say that determines the style in which each of his basic sentences will extend their scope for saying something. The following is a sample of the four sentence styles. The basic sentence in each is underlined, and the verbal element (verb, copula, copular verb) rendered in bold italics:

Simple Sentence Style

The simple sentence is any basic sentence. It is 'simple' because no complex or compound operation happens in it. A few inter-planted adverbs and adjectives do not make a complex sentence of it.

The book is a justifiably angry polemic.

This is a copula basic sentence in which the subject 'book' is assigned the definition 'a polemic' by the copula 'is'. The adjective phrase 'justifiably angry' describes the noun 'polemic'.

Complex Sentence Style

The complex sentence is formed when a basic sentence is embedded by phrases with a variety of syntactic functions. Reopening their battle on the eve of the election, they warned that all candidates will be challenged to oppose the proposed defence cuts. This complex sentence has a copular-verb basic sentence that specifies the content of the act 'warned' of the subject 'they' with the noun phrase 'that all candidates will be challenged to oppose the cuts'.

Compound Sentence Style

The compound sentence conjoins two or more simple sentences by means of logical operators.

It is an annoyance that their writers play historian because there is no more in these stories than ordinary romance.

This compound sentence contains:

(i) a copula basic sentence in which copula 'is' directs the noun phrase 'an annoyance that their writers play historian' to occupy the vacant subject 'It'.

This is compounded by because to:

(ii) the copula basic sentence in which the copula 'is' directs the noun phrase 'no more than romance' to occupy the vacant subject 'there'.

Composite Sentence style

A composite sentence is made up of several sentences that are capable of being spliced by commas. We insist on fresh vegetables, they like strong spicing, their children will eat only chips, so choosing a restaurant is always a problem.

This sentence contains:

(i) a copular-verb basic sentence in which the noun phrase 'on vegetables' locates the direction of the act 'insist' of the subject 'We'.

This is spliced to:

(ii) a verb basic sentence in which the subject 'They' perpetrates the act denoted by 'like' upon the object 'spicing'.

This is spliced to:

(iii) a verb basic sentence in which the subject 'children' perpetrates the act denoted by 'will eat' upon the object 'chips'.

This is spliced by a comma and 'so' to:

(iv) a copula basic sentence in which the copula 'is' assigns the definition 'a problem' to the noun-phrase subject 'choosing a restaurant'.

DEPENDENT SENTENCE

The dependent sentence does not construct its own subject-object/complement unit. It borrows that unit, and the sense it makes, from the independent sentence that precedes it. It is a staple feature of texts that represent dialogue:

'Margaret was married yesterday.'

'I know.'

'You will miss her.'

'Yes.'

Both the sentences 'I know' and 'Yes' depend on the sentences that precedes them: It is only because the sentence 'Margaret was married yesterday' precedes it that 'I know' can make the sense 'I know that Margaret was married yesterday'. And it is only because the sentence 'You will miss her' precedes it that 'Yes' can make the sense 'I will miss her'. The next sentence is not a model of the basic sentence: 'The tall girl'. Yet it raises the subject 'girl' and describes her as 'tall': Doing this, it should be acknowledged as a copula basic sentence. But it is not: The description is not effected by the copula:

The adjective 'tall' is an attributive adjective, not a predicate adjective. Given its text, this sentence reveals itself to be the verb basic sentence 'The tall girl is flying to the moon tomorrow':

'Who is flying to the moon tomorrow?'

'The tall girl.'

The dependent sentence is in no way an inferior sentence. In some texts it is much more appropriate than the independent sentence.

BASIC ENGLISH GRAMMAR

English grammar is a description of the usages of the English language by good speakers and writers of the present day. There are sufficient to suggest several distinct notions about English grammar—

(1) It makes rules to tell us how to use words.

(2) It is a record of usage which we ought to follow.

(3) It is concerned with the forms of the language.

(4) English has no grammar in the sense of forms, or inflections, but takes account merely of the nature and the uses of words in sentences.

Fierce discussions have raged over these opinions, and numerous works have been written to uphold the theories. The first of them remained popular for a very long time. It originated from the etymology of the word grammar and from an effort to build up a treatise on English grammar by using classical grammar as a model. Perhaps a combination of (1) and (3) has been still more popular, though there has been vastly more classification than there are forms. During recent years, (2) and (4) have been gaining ground, but they have had hard work to displace the older and more popular theories. It is insisted by many that the student's time should be used in studying general literature, and thus learning the fluent and correct use of his mother tongue. It is also insisted that the study and discussion of forms and inflections is an inexcusable imitation of classical treatises.

The province of English grammar is, rightly considered, wider than is indicated by any one of the above definitions; and the student ought to have a clear idea of the ground to be covered. It must be admitted that the language has very few inflections at present, as compared with Latin or Greek; so that a small grammar will hold them all.

It is also evident, to those who have studied the language historically, that it is very hazardous to make rules in grammar: what is at present regarded as correct may not be so twenty years from now, even if our rules are founded on the keenest scrutiny of the "standard" writers of our time. Usage is varied as our way of thinking changes.

Grammar is eminently a means of mental training; and while it will train the student in subtle and acute reasoning, it will at the same time, if rightly presented, lay the foundation of a keen observation and a correct literary taste. The continued contact with the highest thoughts of the best minds will create a thirst for the "well of English undefiled."

English grammar is the science which treats of the nature of words, their forms, and their uses and relations in the sentence. This will take in the usual divisions, "The Parts of Speech" (with their inflections), "Analysis," and "Syntax. " It will also require a discussion of any points that will clear up difficulties, assist the classification of kindred expressions, or draw the attention of the student to everyday idioms and phrases, and thus incite his observation.

In order to speak and write the English language correctly, it is imperative that the fundamental principles of the Grammar be mastered, for no matter how much we may read of the best authors, no matter how much we may associate with and imitate the best speakers.

If we do not know the underlying principles of the correct formation of sentences and the relation of words to one another, we will be to a great extent like the parrot, that merely repeats what it hears without understanding the import of what is said.

Letters

A *letter* is a mark or character used to represent an articulate sound. Letters are divided into *vowels* and *consonants*. A vowel is a letter which makes a distinct sound by itself. Consonants cannot be sounded without the aid of vowels. The vowels are *a, e, i, o, u,* and sometimes *w* and *y* when they do not begin a word or syllable.

Syllables and Words

A syllable is a distinct sound produced by a single effort of [Transcriber's note: 1-2 words illegible] shall, pig, dog. In every syllable there must be at least one vowel. A word consists of one syllable or a combination of syllables. Many rules are given for the dividing of words into syllables, but the best is to follow as closely as possible the divisions made by the organs of speech in properly pronouncing them.

PARTS OF SPEECH

Article

An *Article* is a word placed before a noun to show whether the noun is used in a particular or general sense. English has two types of articles: definite (the) and indefinite (a, an.) The use of these articles depends mainly on whether you are referring to any member of a group, or to a specific member of a group:

Indefinite articles: a *and* an

A and *an* signal that the noun modified is indefinite, referring to *any* member of a group. These indefinite articles are used with singular nouns when the noun is general; the corresponding indefinite quantity word *some* is used for plural general nouns. The rule is:

— a + singular noun beginning with a consonant: *a boy*

— an + singular noun beginning with a vowel: *an elephant*

— a + singular noun beginning with a consonant sound: *a user* (sounds like 'yoo-zer,' i.e. begins with a consonant 'y' sound, so 'a' is used)

— some + plural noun: *some girls*

If the noun is modified by an adjective, the choice between *a* and *an* depends on the initial sound of the adjective that immedately follows the article:

— *a* broken egg

— *an* unusual problem

— a European country (sounds like 'yer-o-pi-an,' i.e. begins with consonant 'y' sound)

Note also that in English, the indefinite articles are used to indicate membership in a profession, nation, or religion.

— I am *a* teacher.

— Brian is *an* Irishman.

— Seiko is *a* practicing Buddhist.

Definite article: the

The definite article is used before singular and plural nouns when the noun is particular or specific. *The* signals that the noun is definite, that it refers to a *particular* member of a group. Compare the indefinite and definite articles in the following examples:

	Indefinite (*a* or *an*)	Definite (*the*)
Singular	*a* dog (any dog)	*an* apple (any apple)
	the dog (that specific dog)	*the* apple (that specific apple)
Plural	*some* dogs (any dogs)	*some* apples (any apples)
	the dogs (those specific dogs)	*the* apples (those specific apples)

The is not used with noncountable nouns referring to something in a general sense:

[no article] Coffee is a popular drink.

[no article] Japanese was his native language.

[no article] Intelligence is difficult to quantify.

The is used with noncountable nouns that are made more specific by a limiting modifying phrase or clause:

The coffee in my cup is too hot to drink.
The Japanese he speaks is often heard in the countryside.
The intelligence of animals is variable but undeniable.

The is also used when a noun refers to something unique:

the White House

the theory of relativity

the 2006 budget

Do not use *the* before:

— names of countries (Italy, Mexico, Bolivia) except the Netherlands and the US

— names of cities, towns, or states (Seoul, Manitoba, Miami)

— names of streets (Washington Blvd., Main St.)

— names of lakes and bays (Lake Titicaca, Lake Erie) except with a group of lakes like the Great Lakes

— names of mountains (Mount Everest, Mount Fuji) except with ranges of mountains like the Andes or the Rockies or unusual names like the Matterhorn

— names of continents (Asia, Europe)

— names of islands (Easter Island, Maui, Key West)

except with island chains like the Aleutians, the Hebrides, or the Canary Islands

Do use *the* before:

- names of rivers, oceans and seas (the Nile, the Pacific)
- points on the globe (the Equator, the North Pole)
- geographical areas (the Middle East, the West)
- deserts, forests, gulfs, and peninsulas (the Sahara, the Persian Gulf, the Black Forest, the Iberian Peninsula)

4

Improving Your Reading Skills

Good readers understand the processes involved in reading and consciously control them. This awareness and control of the reading processes is called metacognition, which means "knowing about knowing." Some students don't know when they don't know. They continue to read even though they are not comprehending. Poor readers tolerate such confusion because they either don't realise that it exists or don't know what to do about it. Poor readers focus on facts, whereas good readers try to assimilate details into a larger cognitive pattern.

FIVE THINKING STRATEGIES

1. *Predict*: Make educated guesses. Good readers make predictions about thoughts, events, outcomes, and conclusions. As you read, your predictions are confirmed or denied. If they prove invalid, you make new predictions. This constant process helps you become involved with the author's thinking and helps you learn.
2. *Picture*: Form images. For good readers, the words and the ideas on the page trigger mental images that relate directly or indirectly to the

material. Images are like movies in your head, and they increase your understanding of what you read.

3. *Relate*: Draw comparisons. When you relate your existing knowledge to the new information in the text, you are embellishing the material and making it part of your framework of ideas. A phrase of a situation may remind you of a personal experience or something that you read or saw in a film. Such related experiences help you digest the new material.

4. *Monitor*: Check understanding. Monitor your ongoing comprehension to test your understanding of the material. Keep an internal summary or synthesis of the information as it is presented and how it relates to the overall message. Your summary will build with each new detail, and as long as the message is consistent, you will continue to form ideas. If, however, certain information seems confusing or erroneous, you should stop and seek a solution to the problem. You must monitor and supervise you own comprehension. Good readers seek to resolve difficulties when they occur; they do not keep reading when they are confused.

5. *Correct gaps in understanding*: Do not accept gaps in your reading comprehension. They may signal a failure to understand a word or a sentence. Stop and resolve the problem. Seek solutions, not confusion. This may mean rereading a sentence or looking back at a previous page for clarification. If an unknown word is causing confusion, the definition may

emerge through further reading. When good readers experience gaps in comprehension, they do not perceive themselves as failures; instead, they reanalyse the task to achieve better understanding.

People just aren't reading as much anymore and yet the need for reading, comprehension, and communication skills (verbal and written) has increased. The need is great for strengthening the following skills:

- Your ability to read a variety of materials (e.g. textbooks, novels, newspapers, magazines, instructional manuals).
- Your ability to understand and remember what you read.
- Your ability to effectively communicate what you've learned from your reading.

MOTIVATIONAL GOALS

Engaged, active readers have deep-seated motivational goals, which include being committed to the subject matter, wanting to learn the content, believing in one's own ability, and wanting to share understandings from learning. However, most people, children and adults, do not spend any significant portion of their free time reading. Without committing time to reading, no one can gain the reading skills or knowledge they need to succeed in school, at work, or in life in general. The best way to improve your reading efficiency is to read a lot.

READING COMPREHENSION

According to Webster's Dictionary, comprehension is

"the capacity for understanding fully; the act or action of grasping with the intellect." Webster also tells us that reading is "to receive or take in the sense of (as letters or symbols) by scanning; to understand the meaning of written or printed matter; to learn from what one has seen or found in writing or printing.

Identifying words on a page does not make someone a successful reader. When the words are understood and transcend the pages to become thoughts and ideas then you are truly reading. Comprehension therefore is the capacity for understanding those thoughts and ideas. Applying what you have read and understood becomes the successful conclusion. When you comprehend what you read it is like taking a trip around the world, staying as long as you like, visiting all the places you wish, and you never even having to pack a suitcase! Reading can be an escape that takes you outside the bounds of your existence. Reading is your ticket to whatever you choose to do and become. Reading is your future as well as your past. Don't be a reader who reads without thinking or who reads without a purpose.

Comprehension Regulation

You can become an active, effective reader through comprehension regulation. This is a method for consciously controlling the reading process. Comprehension regulation involves the use of preplanned strategies to understand text. It is a plan for getting the most out of reading. It allows you to have an idea of what to expect from the text. Most importantly, it gives you techniques to use when you are experiencing difficulties.

As an active reader, you can get an idea of what the writer is trying to communicate by:

- Setting goals based on your purpose for reading
- Previewing the text to make predictions
- Self-questioning
- Scanning
- Relating new information to old

There are many different purposes for reading. Sometimes you read a text to learn material, sometimes you read for pure pleasure, and sometimes you need to follow a set of directions. As a student, much of your reading will be to learn assigned material. You get information from everything you read and yet you don't read everything for the same reason or in the same way or at the same rate. Each purpose or reason for reading requires a different reading approach. Two things that influence how fast and how well you read are the characteristics of the text and the characteristics of you, the reader.

Characteristics of the text:

- Size and style of the type (font)
- Pictures and illustrations
- Author's writing style and personal perspectives
- Difficulty of the ideas presented

Characteristics of the reader:

- Background knowledge (how much you already know about the material or related concepts)

- Reading ability - vocabulary and comprehension
- Interest
- Attitude

Skills for being an effective reader and for increasing comprehension are:

- Finding main ideas and supporting details/ evidence
- Making inferences and drawing conclusions
- Recognising a text's patterns of organisation
- Perceiving conceptual relationships
- Testing your knowledge and understanding of the material through application

When comprehension fails, or your understanding seems limited, you can use a plan that includes:

- Using structural analysis and contextual clues to identify unknown vocabulary words. If this fails, keep a dictionary close by and look up words you don't understand
- Reading more critically - ask questions while you read
- Summarising or outlining main points and supporting details
- Rereading the material
- Do a "think aloud" and/or try to explain what you've read to someone else

Although, reading means different things to different people and skills vary with every individual, reading is a skill that can be improved. Students from various backgrounds are in reading courses for a variety of reasons. Weaknesses in vocabulary, comprehension, speed, or a combination of all three may be the result of ineffective reading habits. Active reading is engaged reading and can be achieved through comprehension regulation strategies.

LEVELS OF READING COMPREHENSION

Reading is a thinking activity. By now you have read this several times...is it sinking in?_____ This process involves getting meaning from the printed word or symbol. College instructors will expect that you, as a college student, will be able to read at all levels of meaning or comprehension. In this case, LEVELS mean different depths of understanding, different analysis of what is meant. In other words, you will be expected to read at different levels of comprehension. These three different levels of comprehension can be called the literal level, the interpretive level and the applied level. Let's examine what each means briefly.

Literal Level

The first level of comprehension can be called the literal level for the sake of wording because it is the most simple. At this level, you would not have to understand the true meaning of a paragraph, however, you could memorise the information. Instructors might ask you to read a chapter dealing with dates or specific facts. At the literal level, you would memorise these dates and facts. However, even though you have memorised these facts, this does not mean that you necessarily understand their full meaning or see the implication of these dates and facts applied to other situations. At the literal level, you are looking at what was written by an author at "face value", little interpretation is needed.

Let's suppose you are taking a history course to satisfy a humanities credit...say, HIS 101 or HIS 102 (Western Civilisation). Now let's examine this more carefully. If you memorised that King Henry VIII ascended the throne of England in 1509...knowing this date does NOT make you a historian! On the contrary, all through our lives we have memorised various dates and specific facts. The memorisation of these facts does not make us an expert necessarily, but it does allow us to recall information. Let's take another example at the literal level. This time, let's use mathematics as the example. At some point in you school career, you probably were exposed to this math formula: $kr^2 = A$ This is stated: pi r squared = Area.

If you do not know what it means, you could memorise that the symbol k (pi) stands for the 16th letter of the Greek alphabet representing the value found by dividing the diameter of a circle into its circumference. Now if that is not confusing enough, suppose that your instructor said, "Memorise the formula, never mind what it exactly means!" You would be forced to memorise it and be able to put the numerical values into the formula to find the solution to "A." Oh by the way, this formula is used to find the area of a circle! The point of all of this is that at the literal level of comprehension, you are at the most basic of levels. You are building your knowledge but you do not necessarily have command of it.

Interpretive Level

The second level of comprehension is called the interpretive level. At this level, you are attempting to understand what the author meant by what s/he said in the story, paragraph or textbook. It is presumed that you have already memorised certain facts at the literal level and now you are attempting to see the implications of the author's words. At this level, you are attempting to "read between the lines." as they say. At this level, you are attempting to understand that which you memorised at the literal level of comprehension

Instead of looking at the facts concerning when King Henry VIII ascended the throne of England, perhaps now you are attempting to understand the social implications and the political implications of his ascension to the throne. Perhaps a teacher might ask you, "How did King Henry VIII wield his power as King of England?"

This question is decidedly more complex than the previous one, where you are ONLY asked to report what year he became King. This new question about "how" he wielded his power would force you to understand more than the date that he became King. Knowing the how's and why's behind this level of understanding is obviously a much deeper or profound level of thinking. Interestingly, it is this level of comprehension that college instructors will most likely expect you to get to in their courses. Of course they want you to "memorise" dates, facts, details, but they also want you to be able to understand how that information relates to and is connected to the "bigger picture" of what you are studying.

Now, refer to the math formula problem from the literal level section again. At the interpretive level, you would be able to understand this formula "pi r squared" and know how it could be proven or perhaps be aware of its implication to you the math student. The levels of reading comprehension have implications for learning that stretch across disciplines, across ways of learning, and can allow us access to information when we are trying to build our "learning curve."

Your ability to address the question from the King Henry VIII problem is hinged on your ability to make your learning curve grow! As you study and learn the facts, then and only then, can you "explain" yourself when it comes time for a test or an exam. Then and only then, can you see the implications about a certain concept. Then and only then, can you prove that pi times the radius squared does indeed equal the area of a circle! Understanding the implications of an idea is like "reading between the lines," as has already been mentioned.

Applied Level

The last level is called the applied level. At this level the reader or student can attempt to answer this question: Question: How would the author's message apply to other situations given what you memorised and understood at the other two levels? At this level, you are attempting to elevate or raise your thinking one more "notch" or level to a more critical, analysing level. This presumes that you have already reached the previous two levels. At this level, you are "reading between the lines" and then examining the message from the author and attempting to apply that message to other settings.

For example, still following the ideas about King Henry VIII, what if the history professor lectured on "power," the power that monarchs have, assume, take control of, etc. In that discussion, if s/he asked you to consider this question, think about how you would respond: How does power affect a person?

In this pretend scenario from history, a student started at the literal level memorising dates from history. At the interpretive level, the student would have examined the implications of those dates...what else was going on, what impact King Henry might have had on England, on the politics of the time, etc. At the applied level, the student has now spent a fair amount of time building his/her learning curve and is now more able to see the larger implications of people who either are born "powerful" by their lineage of birth or have assumed power like someone elected into office. Either way, if an instructor asks you to write an essay explaining how people are affected (controlled or influenced) by power and you responded appropriately...you would be at the applied level of comprehension.

Reading Rate

"Reading well" does not mean reading everything at the same pace and with the same technique. As a college student, much of your reading will be assigned material. You get information from everything you read and yet you don't read everything for the same reason or in the same way. For example, a novel can be read quickly just to get the story, whereas a poem might be read slowly, perhaps several times to determine the meaning. Good readers are flexible readers. Once they determine their purpose for reading, they adjust their rate to fit the type of material they are reading.

Five Categories

- Careful - used to master content including details, evaluate material, outline, summarise, paraphrase, analyse, solve problems, memorise, evaluate literary value or read poetry.
- Normal - used to answer a specific question, note details, solve problems, read material of average difficulty, understand relationship of details to main ideas, appreciate beauty or literary style, keep up with current events, or read with the intention of later retelling what you have read.
- Rapid - used to review familiar material, get the main idea or central thought, retrieve information for short-term use, read light material for relaxation or pleasure or comprehend the basic plot.
- Scanning - the method by which you read the newspaper - used to get an overview of the content or to preview.
- Skimming - done a little more quickly. It is what you do when you are searching for something particular in the text—the way you might read a phone book or dictionary. Used to find a specific

reference, locate new material, locate the answer to a specific question, get the main idea of a selection, or review.

Knowing how to use all five reading styles is a great advantage to you because it gives you a wide variety of ways to handle your reading. It also gives you choices, and the more choices you have, the more power you have to arrange your life in satisfying ways.

Textbook Reading

The following strategy, SQ4R, is built around the idea that what you do before and after you read is as important as the reading itself. Learning is an active process which requires concentration and energy. Understanding and using the following strategies will increase your comprehension and your retention of the information.

Survey

Look over a chapter for a few minutes before studying it in depth.

- Read the title and introductory paragraph(s). Fix the name of the chapter in your mind. Often the introduction to the chapter supplies background for recognising the purpose of the chapter. It may also state specifically the method of development the author intends to follow.
- Read headings, subheadings, and italicised words. Go through the chapter heading by heading; these will form a topical outline.
- Read the summary at the end of the chapter. Reread it to see which ideas the author restates

for special emphasis or what general conclusions he or she comes to. If there is no summary, read the last sentence or two before each new heading.

Before reading

— Use the chapter survey to activate your prior knowledge of the subject. Recall what you already know about the subject by trying to anticipate the chapter's main points.
— Use the chapter survey to predict the predominant thought patterns.
— Use surveying to anticipate which portions or sections of the chapter will be most difficult or challenging.

While reading

— Use the survey as a guide to what is important to learn.
— Highlight, mark or underline key information mentioned in the survey.

After reading

— Use the survey to monitor the effectiveness of your reading.
— Test your ability to recall the key information.
— Review immediately any material you were unable to recall.

Question

Formulate questions in before you read the material.

- Turn each heading and subtitle into a question. Form questions from all three sections of the "Levels of Comprehension" attached at the end of the packet (Who? What? When? Where? Why? How?). You should be able to answer these questions when you finish reading and studying the paragraph, section, or chapter.
- Restate the questions from headings to help fix them in your mind. These questions give purpose to your reading. Remember that reading is thinking, and good students think while they read.

Read

Read the material.

- Read only the material covered under one heading or subheading at a time, and look for the answers to your questions.
- Read ideas, not just words.
- Take only minimal notes while reading.
- Read aggressively, with the intent of getting answers, of noting supporting details, and of remembering.
- Apply the 50/10 rule for studying; read for 50 minutes and then take a 10 minute break. You will be able to sustain longer study times with better concentration and retention.

Recite

Do "question-read-recite" for each subheading.

- Answer the questions that you raised before you began to read. Answer fully, and be sure to include the reasons the author believes the answer is true. Recall the answer and do not refer to the book.

- Tell yourself the major concept(s) of the section. Put the ideas into your own words. If you simply read a textbook chapter, you will probably remember less than one-third of what you read by the following week. In two months, you will remember about 14 % of the material, hardly enough to do well on a test. In order to transfer a greater portion of the material you read from your short-term to long-term memory, you must do something active with the information to help "attach" it to your memory. If you take time after reading each section of the chapter to recite the information, you will ensure that more of it goes into long-term memory. If you recite, you are likely to remember 80 % of what you read after a week and 70 % after two months. Now check your answers by referring to the book.

Record

Take notes from the reading.

- After having read a section and reflected on what you have read and questioned yourself about the material, you are ready to take notes. Taking notes at this point in time will almost ensure that you are noting the important parts of the section. Go back over the paragraphs and highlight or underline only the main ideas and supporting details with no more than 10-15% of the page highlighted. Use marginal notations as a way to separate main ideas from examples and each of those from new terminology.

Review

Review the material.

- Look over your notes and the headings and subheadings in the text. Get an overall view of the main points.
- Recall supporting details under each main point.
- Predict test questions based on these main points, especially questions which would fall into the critical and creative levels of reading comprehension. Try true/false and completion-type questions from details. Essay questions are easy to make from the main headings. Answer your test questions.

ORGANISATIONAL PATTERNS OF PARAGRAPHS

Basic Unit of Thought

Perhaps one of the best ways to improve your reading ability is to learn to read paragraphs effectively. Many experts believe the paragraph, not the sentence, is the basic unit of thought of a selection. If one can quickly grasp the meaning of each of these though units while reading, then comprehension will be heightened. It is important to identify with the author's perspective by discovering the way the message is being sent.

Every writer has a purpose for writing and some plan of action for getting a message across. This plan of action is the order in which the material will be presented in the text. This order, often called a pattern of organisation, should be present in acceptable writing from the smallest to the largest unit of writing: the paragraph, groups of paragraphs, sub-chapters, chapters, groups of chapters, whole books, and even series of books. Each of these, then, contains a certain pattern of organisation.

Anticipating the order in which the material will be presented helps you put the facts into perspective and to see how the parts fit into the whole. For example, if the selection begins by indicating that there are four important components of management, you are alert to look for four key phrases to mark and remember.

Likewise, if a comparison is suggested, you want to note the points that are similar in nature. For material that shows cause and effect, you need to anticipate the linkage and note the relationship.

The importance of these patterns is that they signal how the facts will be presented. They are blueprints for you to use. In textbook reading the number of details can be overwhelming. The mind responds to logical patterns; relating the small parts to the whole simplifies complexities of the material and makes remembering easier.

Although key signal words help in identifying the particular type of pattern, a single paragraph can be a mixture of different patterns. Your aim is to anticipate the overall pattern and then place the facts into a broad perspective. The following six examples are the patterns of organisation that are most frequently found in textbooks.

Simple Listing

Items are randomly listed in a series of supporting facts or details. These supporting elements are of equal value, and the order in which they are presented is of no importance. Changing the order of the items does not change the meaning of the paragraph.

Signal words often used for simple listing are:

. in addition	. also
. another	. several
. for example	. a number of

Description

Description is like listing; the characters that make up a description are no more than a simple listing of details.

Definition

Frequently in textbook reading an entire paragraph is devoted to defining a complex term or idea. The concept is initially defined and then further expanded with examples and restatements.

Signal words often used for definition are:

. is defined as	. is called
. means	. refers to
. is described as	. term or concept

Chronological (Time) Order

Items are listed in the order in which they occurred or in a specifically planned order in which they must develop. In this case, the order is important and changing it would change the meaning.

Signal words often used for chronological order or sequence are:

- first, second, third
- before, after
- when
- later
- until
- at last
- next

Comparison

Items are related by the comparisons (similarities) that are made or by the contrasts (differences) that are prêsented. The author's purpose is to show similarities and differences.

Signal words often used for comparison-contrast are:

- similar, different
- on the other hand
- but
- however
- bigger than, smaller than
- in the same way
- parallels

Cause and Effect

In this pattern, one item is showed as having produced another element. An event (effect) is said to have happened because of some situation or circumstance (cause). The cause (the action) stimulates the event, or effect (the outcome).

Signal words often used for cause and effect are:

- for this reason
- consequently
- on that acount
- hence
- because
- made

IDENTIFYING TOPICS AND SUPPORTING DETAILS

Understanding the topic, the gist, or the larger conceptual framework of a textbook chapter, an article, a paragraph, a sentence or a passage is a sophisticated reading task. Being able to draw conclusions, evaluate, and critically interpret articles or chapters is important for overall comprehension in college reading. Textbook chapters, articles, paragraphs, sentences, or passages all have topics and main ideas.

The topic is the broad, general theme or message. It is what some call the subject. The main idea is the "key concept" being expressed. Details, major and minor, support the main idea by telling how, what, when, where, why, how much, or how many. Locating the topic, main idea, and supporting details helps you understand the point(s) the writer is attempting to express. Identifying the relationship between these will increase your comprehension.

Applying Strategy

The successful communication of any author's topic is only as good as the organisation the author uses to build and define his/her subject matter.

Grasping the main idea

A paragraph is a group of sentences related to a particular topic, or central theme. Every paragraph has a key concept or main idea. The main idea is the most important piece of information the author wants you to know about the concept of that paragraph. When authors write they have an idea in mind that they are trying to get across. This is especially true as authors compose paragraphs. An author organises each paragraph's main idea and supporting details in support of the topic or central theme, and each paragraph supports the paragraph preceding it.

A writer will state his/her main idea explicitly somewhere in the paragraph. That main idea may be stated at the beginning of the paragraph, in the middle, or at the end. The sentence in which the main idea is stated is the topic sentence of that paragraph. The topic sentence announces the general theme (or portion of the theme) to be dealt with in the paragraph. Although the topic sentence may appear anywhere in the paragraph, it is usually first—and for a very good reason. This sentence provides the focus for the writer while writing and for the reader while reading. When you find the topic sentence, be sure to underline it so that it will stand out not only now, but also later when you review.

Identifying the topic

The first thing you must be able to do to get at the main idea of a paragraph is to identify the topic—the subject of the paragraph. Think of the paragraph as a wheel with the topic being the hub—the central core around which the whole wheel spins. Your strategy for topic identification is simply to ask yourself the question, "What is this about?" Keep asking yourself that question as you read a paragraph, until the answer to your question becomes clear. Sometimes you can spot the topic by looking for a word or two that repeat. Usually you can state the topic in a few words.

Let us try this topic-finding strategy. Reread the first paragraph on this page—the first paragraph under the heading Grasping the Main Idea. Ask yourself the question, "What is this paragraph about?" To answer, say to yourself in your mind, "The author keeps talking about paragraphs and the way they are designed. This must be the topic—paragraph organisation." Reread the second paragraph of the same section. Ask yourself "What is this paragraph about?" Did you say to yourself, "This paragraph is about different ways to organise a paragraph"? That is the topic. Next, reread the third paragraph and see if you can find the topic of the paragraph. How? Write the topic in the margin next to this paragraph. Remember, getting the main idea of a paragraph is crucial to reading.

The bulk of an expository paragraph is made up of supporting sentences, which help to explain or prove the main idea. These sentences present facts, reasons, examples, definitions, comparison, contrasts, and other pertinent details. They are most important because they sell the main idea. The last sentence of a paragraph is likely to be a concluding sentence. It is used to sum up a discussion, to emphasize a point, or to restate all or part of the topic sentence so as to bring the paragraph to a close. The last sentence may also be a transitional sentence leading to the next paragraph.

Of course, the paragraphs you'll be reading will be part of some longer piece of writing—a textbook chapter, a section of a chapter, or a newspaper or magazine article. Besides expository paragraphs, in which new information is presented and discussed, these longer writings contain three types of paragraphs: introductory, transitional, and summarising.

Introductory paragraphs tell you, in advance, such things as

(1) the main ideas of the chapter or section;

(2) the extent or limits of the coverage;

(3) how the topic is developed; and

(4) the writer's attitude toward the topic.

Transitional paragraphs are usually short; their sole function is to tie together what you have read so far and what is to come—to set the stage for succeeding ideas of the chapter or section. Summarising paragraphs are used to restate briefly the main ideas of the chapter or section. The writer may also draw some conclusion from these ideas, or speculate on some conclusion based on the evidence he/she has presented. All three types should alert you: the introductory paragraph of things to come; the transitional paragraph of a new topic; and the summarising paragraph of main ideas that you should have getting.

MAKING INFERENCES AND DRAWING CONCLUSIONS

Read with Purpose and Meaning

Drawing conclusions refers to information that is implied or inferred. This means that the information is never clearly stated. Writers often tell you more than they say directly. They give you hints or clues that help you "read between the lines." Using these clues to give you a deeper understanding of your reading is called inferring. When you infer, you go beyond the surface details to see other meanings that the details suggest or imply (not stated). When the meanings of words are not stated clearly in the context of the text, they may be implied—that is, suggested or hinted at. When meanings are implied, you may infer them.

Inference is just a big word that means a conclusion or judgement. If you infer that something has happened, you do not see, hear, feel, smell, or taste the actual event. But from what you know, it makes sense to think that it has happened. You make inferences everyday. Most of the time you do so without thinking about it. Suppose you are sitting in your car stopped at a red signal light. You hear screeching tires, then a loud crash and breaking glass. You see nothing, but you infer that there has been a car accident. We all know the sounds of screeching tires and a crash.

We know that these sounds almost always mean a car accident. But there could be some other reason, and therefore another explanation, for the sounds. Perhaps it was not an accident involving two moving vehicles. Maybe an angry driver rammed a parked car. Or maybe someone played the sound of a car crash from a recording. Making inferences means choosing the most likely explanation from the facts at hand. There are several ways to help you draw conclusions from what an author may be implying. The following are descriptions of the various ways to aid you in reaching a conclusion.

Antonyms and Contrasts

When the meaning of a word is not implied by the general sense of its context or by examples, it may be implied by an antonym or by a contrasting thought in a context. Antonyms are words that have opposite meanings, such as happy and sad. For instance, Ben is fearless, but his brother is timorous. You may infer the meaning of timorous by answering the question "If Ben is fearless and Jim is very different from Ben with regard to fear, then what word describes Jim?" Write your answer on the following line. If you wrote a word such as timid, or afraid, or fearful, you inferred the meaning of timorous.

A contrast in the following sentence implies the meaning of credence:

> Dad gave credence to my story, but Mom's reaction was one of total disbelief.
>
> You may infer the meaning of credence by answering the question "If Mom's reaction was disbelief and Dad's reaction was very different from Mom's, what was Dad's reaction?" Write your answer on the following lines.
>
> If you wrote that Dad believed the story, you correctly inferred the meaning of credence; it means "belief."

Be Careful of the Meaning You Infer!

When a sentence contains an unfamiliar word, it is sometimes possible to infer the general meaning of the sentence without inferring the exact meaning of the unknown word. For instance, When we invite the Paulsons for dinner, they never invite us to their home for a meal; however, when we have the Browns to dinner, they always reciprocate.

In reading this sentence some students infer that the Browns are more desirable dinner guests than the Paulsons without inferring the exact meaning of reciprocate. Other students conclude that the Browns differ from the Paulsons in that they do something in return when they are invited for dinner; these students conclude correctly that reciprocate means "to do something in return."

INTERPRETING WHAT YOU READ

Because writers don't always say things directly, sometimes it is difficult to figure out what a writer really means or what he or she is really trying to say. You need to learn to "read between the lines"— to take the information the writer gives you and figure things out for yourself.

You will also need to learn to distinguish between fact and opinion. Writers often tell us what they think or how they feel, but they don't always give us the facts. It's important to be able to interpret what the writer is saying so you can form opinions of your own. As you read an author's views, you should ask yourself if the author is presenting you with an established fact or with a personal opinion. Since the two may appear close together, even in the same sentence, you have to be able to distinguish between them.

The key difference between facts and opinions is that facts can be verified, or checked for accuracy, by anyone. In contrast, opinions cannot be checked for accuracy by some outside source. Opinions are what someone personally thinks or how he/she feel about an issue. Opinions by definition are subjective and relative.

Defining A Fact

Facts are objective, concrete bits of information. They can be found in official government and legal records, and in the physical sciences. Facts can be found in reference books, such as encyclopedias and atlases, textbooks, and relevant publications. Objective facts are what researchers seek in laboratories or through controlled studies. Facts are usually expressed by precise numbers or quantities, in weights and measures, and in concrete language.

The decisions of Congress, specific technological data, birth records, historical documents, all provide researchers with reliable facts. Since anyone can look up facts, facts are generally not the subject of disputes. However, not all facts are absolutes. Often the problem is that facts are simply not readily available—such as battles like the Little/Big Horn where all the witnesses who could give information on what happened died in the disaster.

In 1876, Lieutenant Colonel George Armstrong Custer and his 7th Cavalry engaged in a fight with Sioux Indians along the Little/Big Horn Rivers in Montana. Custer and his entire company were wiped out; no one survived to tell what really happened. In this instance, we can only read opinions on how this disaster befell Custer.

To sum up, facts

— can be verified in reference books, official records, and so forth.

- are expressed in concrete language or specific numbers.
- once verified, are generally agreed upon by people.

Determining An Opinion

Opinions are based on subjective judgment and personal values rather than on information that can be verified. An opinion is a belief that someone holds without complete proof or positive knowledge that it is correct. Even experts who have studied the same issue carefully often have very different opinions about that issue.

Opinions are often disputed, and many times involve abstract concepts and complex moral issues such as right or wrong, fairness and loyalty. Abstract concepts, because they are not easily understood, can never be defined to everyone's satisfaction. For example, each of us holds a personal opinion about what fairness or loyalty is, about gun control and abortion, and these issues always remain a matter of opinion, not fact.

Although opinions cannot be verified for accuracy, writers should, nevertheless, back their opinions with evidence, facts, and reason—by whatever information supports the opinion and convinces the reader that it is a valid opinion. A valid opinion is one in which the writer's support for his or her opinion is solid and persuasive, and one in which the writer cites other respected authorities who are in agreement. If a writer presents an extreme or unconvincing opinion, the reader should remain wary or unconvinced.

Writers often slip their personal opinions into a piece of writing, even when it is suppose to be a "factual" account; alert readers can identify subjective opinions by studying the writer's language.

— Opinions are often expressed as comparisons (more, strongest, less, most, least efficient, but):

The painter Pablo Picasso was far more innovative than any of his contemporaries.

— Opinions are often expressed by adjectives (brilliant, vindictive, fair, trustworthy):

Ronald Reagan was a convincing speaker when he read a prepared address but was not effective at press conferences.

— Opinions often involve evaluations:

The excellence of her science project was a model for other students.

— Opinions are often introduced by verbs and adverbs that suggest some doubt in the writer's mind:

— It appears she was confused.

— She seems to have the qualifications for the position.

— They probably used dirty tricks to win.

Some opinions obviously deserve more attention than others do. When expert economists, such as John Kenneth Galbraith or Paul Volcher, discuss the U.S. economy, their opinions are more informed and therefore more reliable than the opinions of people who know very little about economic policy. Become an alert and critical reader. Understand the differences between facts and opinions, and interpret and apply both into your critical thinking.

INTERPRETING WHAT YOU READ

Because writers don't always say things directly, sometimes it is difficult to figure out what a writer really means or what he or she is really trying to say. You need to learn to "read between the lines"—to take the information the writer gives you and figure things out for yourself. You will also need to learn to distinguish between fact and opinion. Writers often tell us what they think or how they feel, but they don't always give us the facts.

It's important to be able to interpret what the writer is saying so you can form opinions of your own. As you read an author's views, you should ask yourself if the author is presenting you with an established fact or with a personal opinion. Since the two may appear close together, even in the same sentence, you have to be able to distinguish between them.

The key difference between facts and opinions is that facts can be verified, or checked for accuracy, by anyone. In contrast, opinions cannot be checked for accuracy by some outside source. Opinions are what someone personally thinks or how he/she feel about an issue. Opinions by definition are subjective and relative.

Defining A Fact

Facts are objective, concrete bits of information. They can be found in official government and legal records, and in the physical sciences. Facts can be found in reference books, such as encyclopedias and atlases, textbooks, and relevant publications. Objective facts are what researchers seek in laboratories or through controlled studies. Facts are usually expressed by precise numbers or quantities, in weights and measures, and in concrete language.

The decisions of Congress, specific technological data, birth records, historical documents, all provide researchers with reliable facts. Since anyone can look up facts, facts are generally not the subject of disputes. However, not all facts are absolutes. Often the problem is that facts are simply not readily available—such as battles like the Little/Big Horn where all the witnesses who could give information on what happened died in the disaster.

In 1876, Lieutenant Colonel George Armstrong Custer and his 7th Cavalry engaged in a fight with Sioux Indians along the Little/Big Horn Rivers in Montana. Custer and his entire company were wiped out; no one survived to tell what really happened. In this instance, we can only read opinions on how this disaster befell Custer.

To sum up, facts

- can be verified in reference books, official records, and so forth.
- are expressed in concrete language or specific numbers.
- once verified, are generally agreed upon by people.

Determining An Opinion

Opinions are based on subjective judgment and

personal values rather than on information that can be verified. An opinion is a belief that someone holds without complete proof or positive knowledge that it is correct. Even experts who have studied the same issue carefully often have very different opinions about that issue.

Opinions are often disputed, and many times involve abstract concepts and complex moral issues such as right or wrong, fairness and loyalty. Abstract concepts, because they are not easily understood, can never be defined to everyone's satisfaction.

Although opinions cannot be verified for accuracy, writers should, nevertheless, back their opinions with evidence, facts, and reason—by whatever information supports the opinion and convinces the reader that it is a valid opinion.

A valid opinion is one in which the writer's support for his or her opinion is solid and persuasive, and one in which the writer cites other respected authorities who are in agreement. If a writer presents an extreme or unconvincing opinion, the reader should remain wary or unconvinced.

Writers often slip their personal opinions into a piece of writing, even when it is suppose to be a "factual" account; alert readers can identify subjective opinions by studying the writer's language.

— Opinions are often expressed as comparisons (more, strongest, less, most, least efficient, but):

The painter Pablo Picasso was far more innovative than any of his contemporaries.

- Opinions are often expressed by adjectives (brilliant, vindictive, fair, trustworthy):

Ronald Reagan was a convincing speaker when he read a prepared address but was not effective at press conferences.

- Opinions often involve evaluations:

The excellence of her science project was a model for other students.

- Opinions are often introduced by verbs and adverbs that suggest some doubt in the writer's mind:
  - It appears she was confused.
  - She seems to have the qualifications for the position.
  - They probably used dirty tricks to win.

Some opinions obviously deserve more attention than others do. When expert economists, such as John Kenneth Galbraith or Paul Volcher, discuss the U.S. economy, their opinions are more informed and therefore more reliable than the opinions of people who know very little about economic policy. Similarly, when someone is a specialist on the poet John Keats, that person's opinion of Keat's poems should be given considerable weight. Become an alert and critical reader. Understand the differences between facts and opinions, and interpret and apply both into your critical thinking.

CONCENTRATING AND REMEMBERING

Better Concentration

Any organised attempt on your part to remember

more of what you read involves your ability to concentrate on the material you are reading. Intense concentration increases the time you spend attending to the task, an important element in reading.

Students who are impulsive in their actions often find it difficult to concentrate for any length of time. Likewise, students who are passive in their approach to learning—those who are not actively engaged and thinking about what they are reading—often fail to get involved with the material enough to concentrate for long periods of time. Here are some ways to improve your concentration:

— *Improve your attitude*: Some subjects you will encounter in college may not be of high interest to you. Not only that, some subjects may not seem relevant to your field of study. You must maintain a positive attitude however and realise there is a job to be done! To get your degree, you must pass all these courses, not just the ones you like.

— *Attend to the task:* Concentration is a must for successful reading. Yet many distractions may be encountered which lessen your ability to stick to the task and concentrate for long periods of time. A good idea is to keep a "distraction list" of times you were interrupted from concentrating on your reading. The list may include items such as:

a) type of book being read;

b) number of minutes reading before distraction;

c) type of distraction;

d) amount of time taken by the distraction; and

e) a goal to improve.

Concentration is improved if you study when you are the most alert, least tired and in good physical condition. During your scheduled breaks, get up from your desk and walk around or do something physical for about 10 minutes.

- Establish a purpose - If you first determine a purpose for reading, you then have a reason for thinking as well as for completing the reading assignment. Purpose helps focus your attention and improve your concentration. Write out some questions that pertain to the subject matter you are about to read. For instance, what specifically do you want to know or need to know about this subject? By pre-selecting questions to answer, you become an active participant in the learning/reading process.

- Eliminate emotional stress - Rid yourself of impulsive and avoidance behavior due to overwhelming daily stress by keeping a "blame list." This is a list of all the people, situations, circumstances, etc., that you blame for your avoidance behavior. Your blame list can be a benefit in getting you to face your problems squarely. Today's world is highly complex, technocratic, and impersonal. It is no wonder you feel emotionally stressed and drained at times. If you find yourself in the middle of a brief depression or emotional upheaval, do something physical or any activity that is not mind taxing.

Techniques for Remembering:

— *A push from short-term to long-term memory:* To transfer information from short- term to long-term, permanent memory, the brain has to perform several functions. The brain by nature is a selective organ, committing to permanent memory only those items it deems are absolutely necessary to retain. You must determine what is important and what is just fluff. If the information is important and needs to be stored, you must perform an essential operation to insure transfer into permanent memory. This process is called recitation or verbalisation. You help to transfer the information through the recitation process by repeating the information over and over again, or by summarising the information in your own words. This process of reciting important information enables the brain to permanently store the information. Recitation is the best way to commit large amounts of information to long-term memory.

— *Sorting Information:* Sorting large amounts of information into categories can help you remember information more accurately and retrieve information faster. For instance, suppose you had to learn the following concepts for a business class: tools, labor, trees, wildlife, human resources, minerals, machinery, capital resources, factories, tractors, water, power plants, manpower, natural resource, typewriters.

These concepts would be difficult to learn and remember if you were merely trying to memorise the individual terms. If you sort these terms into major categories, you will place a value on the terms and give them meaning. These individual terms could be held in short-term memory long enough for you to push them into long-term memory by using the recitation process.

— If you stop your reading often to review and categorise, it will be easier to verbalise the information at the end of the reading, thereby, improving your long-termmemory.

— Mnemonic Devices - Mnemonic aids (from the Greek word meaning 'to bring to mind') are specific memory enhancing techniques which can be useful in learning enormous amounts of seemingly unrelated information. Mnemonic devices are best suited for remembering facts and least helpful in the interpretation of facts or in relating learned material to your life situations.

5

How to Speak Better English

Oral communication is the spoken interaction between two or more people. However, what we intend to teach you is that the interaction is far more complex than it seems. Oral communication is composed of multiple elements which, when taken as a whole, result in the success or failure of the interaction. Not everyone is an effective communicator. In order to function successfully academically and professionally, you need to learn effective oral communication skills.

For many, conversational speech comes naturally. However, in more formal speech, effective communication skills are essential. A poorly conducted interview, sales presentation, or legal argument could have ramifications that affect many more people than yourself. By becoming an effective communicator you will be able to conduct yourself in a variety of personal, professional, and academic environments with confidence.

Oral communication is a unique and learned rhetorical skill that requires you to understand what you say and how you say it. Unlike conversational speech, speech in more formal environments does not come naturally. What you will learn is how to critically think about how you present yourself as a speaker in all occasions and then how to function in a variety of speaking environments.

As a speaker there are several elements of oral communication of which you need to be aware in order to learn how to use them to your advantage. Let's begin with a few rudimentary skills for interacting with your audience:

RUDIMENTARY SKILLS

Eye Contact

Maintaining eye contact with your audience is the simplest thing you can do to establish a relationship. Eye contact serves many purposes. First, it establishes that the parties are listening. Second, eye contact indicates receptiveness. If a person is not making eye contact, they are less receptive to what you are about to say. Third, eye contact is a basic expressive form. A speaker can learn a lot from the audience by just reading what their eyes are saying.

Body Language

As a speaker, the messages you send through your body language affect how your audience perceives you. Whether you are interacting oneon- one or with an auditorium of 200 people, the effectiveness of your message is affected by how you carry yourself. For example, when speaking to a large audience, crossing your arms is seen as bad body language. It shows that you, as the speaker, are closed off from the audience, which reflects negatively on your attitude towards the audience and your topic. You want your body language to establish interest and sincerity toward your audience.

Style and Register

Your tone and pace of speech affect how your audience responds to you. You want to match your tone to that of your audience. You do not want to come off as arrogant or ignorant. Rather, you need to sound confident at a basic level so that you do not lose credibility with your audience. The pace of your speech is also important. You can speak faster than you can write and understand. You need to give your audience time to take in what you have just said, or you risk losing your audience.

Understanding Your Audience

Whether you are interacting one-on-one with a friend or coworker or speaking before a large group, understanding your audience is a part of effective communication. Knowing who your audience is allows you to tailor your content. Your audience will have differing levels of knowledge and differing expectations. Take a moment to look at the worksheet to the right. You will be asked to use it in a modified form in just a moment.

Adapting to Your Audience

Now that you know to whom you are speaking, you need to know how best to address them. You need to determine what level of content and tone are appropriate to your audience. If you are dealing with a person one-on-one, you want to be more personal in your tone and demeanour.

Active and Reflective Listening

As a speaker you should always listen to what your audience has to say, whether it is spoken or not. As a speaker you broadcast a variety of verbal and non-verbal cues, as does your audience. Learning how to read and interpret those cues is part of being a successful communicator.

Oral Communication and Your Preceptorship

As part of your preceptorship you may be giving presentations of various types for your class. You could be conducting an exam review session or giving a minilecture in front of your class. No matter the situation, you need to be prepared.

Planning Process

Initial steps

1. *What type of talk is it?* To begin with you need to identify the type of presentation you will be giving. Is it a group discussion? Is it an exam review? Is it a mini-lecture? Each format has differing requirements; a group discussion would be presented very differently from a mini-lecture.
2. *Identify your audience.* You need to know who your audience is. Refer back to the audience adaptation activity on the previous page. The third-grade learning disabled students had radically differing needs than the culinary

students. When leading a discussion or presenting to your class, you should be able to effectively identify your audience. As a member of their classroom you should know what they need.

3. *How much time do you have?* Time is your biggest constraint in presenting. As the presenter, you need to make critical decisions at the beginning as to what to include and what not to include. It is better to have time left at the end than to go overtime. If you leave extra time at the end of your presentation, you have time available to field questions and clarify any missed points.
4. *Content expectations*. You will need to determine, usually in conjunction with your instructor and/or GTA, what specific content you will need to cover. This is important, as you do not want to disseminate misinformation or confuse your class. Your instructor and GTA are invaluable resources because they are experts on the material.

Outlining

There are three primary benefits to outlining:

- First, it provides you, the speaker, with the needed structure and direction to write your presentation. Without it your presentation ends up disjointed and confusing to your audience.
- Second, your outline will help you assess audience comprehension. When you look out at the audience during the presentation and see a sea of dumbfounded faces, you may want to go back and reiterate your previous point.

— Finally, your outline helps out the audience When the content of your presentation is organised into a logical manner, your audience will be better able to follow and understand you. Think of your outline as the blueprint for your presentation. When preparing a full presentation you will need to plan a detailed outline.

Preparing a group discussion or a review session is different, but you will still want to start with an outline. For a discussion, you want a plan of attack. You need to identify what material you are going to cover and prepare your notes in advance. Take a look at the sample exam review outline in the text box on the next page. It includes all the necessary information you, as a discussion leader, will need: textual and lecture material you and your audience will need to review; and all the relevant concepts that need to be covered.

Visual aids

Whether you are leading a discussion or speaking before your entire class, you should consider using visual aids. As a presenter it is your responsibility to reach out to as much of the audience as possible to address the variety of learning styles they may have. There are a few guidelines to designing your visuals. They should be big, they should be simple, they should be clear, and they should be consistent.

— *Keep them big*. Visibility is very important. You have to remember that the people sitting all the way at the back of the lecture hall need to be able to read your visual aids. Your font size should be large, at least 24 points.

- *Keep them simple.* Many of you have had instructors who place full lecture outlines on the overhead. While it makes sure that nobody misses a point, most students end up copying down the outlines verbatim instead of listening to the instructor. Your visuals should include critical diagrams and tables of data, and key points relevant to your discussion. They should not be detailed lecture outlines.
- *Keep them clear.* Your visuals need to be clear. You need to select images that will project well. Usually larger high-resolution images are best. Use simple block style fonts, as they are more readable than script fonts. Additionally, you need to be careful in picking colours when using PowerPoint. Most experts on PowerPoint recommend dark backgrounds with white or yellow text. Remember that some color combinations, such as green and yellow, may not be visible. The text you put on your visuals needs to be quickly understood. If it requires lengthy explanation, then you should reconsider its use.
- *Consistency is key.* Your visuals need to be consistent in format and style. It looks sloppy when visual aids do not have a consistent format. Your audience will respond better when they perceive you as an organised speaker.

Depending on the material in your presentation, you may want to consider working on a demonstration. Especially in the sciences, offering a real-time demonstration of a key principle will help your audience better understand the material.

Handouts

You may also want to consider using handouts as a supplement to your discussion. The same rules apply to handouts as to visual aids. First and foremost, you do not want your audience distracted by your handouts.

If you put a full presentation outline in your handouts, your audience will not pay attention because they know what you are going to say. Instead, you may want to include important figures and data that will be useful for your audience to have in front of them.

Practice

In order to ensure a successful presentation, you should practice several times to feel comfortable with the content and delivery of the material. While there is no set rule as to how many times you should practice, it should be at least more than once. While practicing, you should be looking out for material that seems confusing or difficult to deliver.

The best feedback that you can get is from yourself. Practice as many times as it takes to make you feel comfortable with the material and your delivery. What about stage fright? For many, giving a speech in front of an audience, no matter how large or small, is an intimidating prospect. The best way to overcome stage fright is preparation.

Presenting and evaluation

Now that you have prepared and practiced your presentation, here are some practical tips for presenting.

- Arrive early to make sure your presentation equipment works.
- Make sure you have all of your materials with you: overheads, PowerPoint, handouts, notes etc.
- Check that the room is set up in a manner that makes it comfortable for you to present.
- While speaking, do not stand behind the lectern for the entire speech; move out from behind it.
- Do not pace across the front of the room. Find a comfortable place to stand and move only to change visuals or when it serves to illustrate a transition. As part of your presentation you should be prepared to ask and answer questions. If you have prepared and practiced adequately, your presentation should be successful. Interacting with large groups of people should not be a frightening experience; rather it should be an opportunity for you to sharpen skills that you will use for the rest of your life. One thing that you may find useful is to have a fellow preceptor or a GTA evaluate your discussion or presentation.

As preceptors, you may be responsible for facilitating discussion groups or running exam reviews. You can apply the above communication skills to great effect in both of these situations.

The skills you have developed in preparing in-class presentations can be modified to handle the greater audience interaction demanded by discussion sessions and exam reviews. AYou need to be constantly considering how to involve your audience in the presentation. The goal is to reinforce previously presented material. Since students have heard it in lecture and read it in their readings (both passive learning modes), your goal with your presentation is to engage them more actively. This can be accomplished through the creation of discussion questions and activities that help students apply the concepts they have learned.

IMPORTANCE OF PRONUNCIATION

Spoken English stress the principal elements in a sentence - content words - and quickly glides over the less important words - function words. Nouns, principal verbs, adjectives and adverbs are all content words.

Pronouns, articles, auxiliary verbs, prepositions, conjunctions are function words and are pronounced quickly moving towards the more important words. This quality of quickly gliding over less important words is also known as 'connected speech'.

Rules

Pronouncing every word correctly leads to poor pronunciation. Good pronunciation comes from stressing the right words - this is because English is a time-stressed language. Learn the following rules concerning pronunciation.

— English is considered a stressed language while many other languages are considered syllabic.

— In other languages, such as French or Italian, each syllable receives equal importance (there is stress, but each syllable has its own length).

- English pronunciation focuses on specific stressed words while quickly gliding over the other, non-stressed, words.
- Stressed words are considered content words: Nouns e.g. kitchen, Peter - (most) principle verbs e.g. visit, construct - Adjectives e.g. beautiful, interesting - Adverbs e.g. often, carefully
- Non-stressed words are considered function words: Determiners e.g. the, a - Auxiliary verbs e.g. am, were - Prepositions e.g. before, of - Conjunctions e.g. but, and - Pronouns e.g. they, she
- Read the following sentence aloud: The beautiful Mountain appeared transfixed in the distance.
- Read the following sentence aloud: He can come on Sundays as long as he doesn't have to do any homework in the evening.
- Notice that the first sentence actually takes about the same time to speak well!
- Even though the second sentence is approximately 30% longer than the first, the sentences take the same time to speak. This is because there are 5 stressed words in each sentence.
- Write down a few sentences, or take a few example sentences from a book or exercise.
- First underline the stressed words, then read aloud focusing on stressing the underlined words and gliding over the non-stressed words.
- Be surprised at how quickly your pronunciation improves! By focusing on stressed words, non-

stressed words and syllables take on their more muted nature.

- When listening to native speakers, focus on how those speakers stress certain words and begin to copy this.
- Remember that non-stressed words and syllables are often "swallowed" in English.
- Always focus on pronouncing stressed words well, non-stressed words can be glided over.
- Don't focus on pronouncing each word. Focus on the stressed words in each sentence.

Intonation and Stress

Say this sentence aloud and count how many seconds it takes.

> *The beautiful Mountain appeared transfixed in the distance.*

Time required? Probably about 5 seconds. Now, try speaking this sentence aloud.

> *He can come on Sundays as long as he doesn't have to do any homework in the evening.*

Time required? Probably about 5 seconds. Wait a minute the first sentence is much shorter than the second sentence!

> *The beautiful Mountain appeared transfixed in the distance. He can come on Sundays as long as he doesn't have to do any homework in the evening*

English is considered a stressed language while many other languages are considered syllabic. What does that mean? It means that, in English, we give stress to certain words while other words are quickly spoken (some students say eaten!). In other languages, such as French or Italian, each syllable receives equal importance (there is stress, but each syllable has its own length).

Many speakers of syllabic languages don't understand why we quickly speak, or swallow, a number of words in a sentence. In syllabic languages each syllable has equal importance, and therefore equal time is needed. English however, spends more time on specific stressed words while quickly gliding over the other, less important, words. Let's look at a simple example: the modal verb "can". When we use the positive form of "can" we quickly glide over the can and it is hardly pronounced.

They can come on Friday. (stressed words underlined)

On the other hand, when we use the negative form "can't" we tend to stress the fact that it is the negative form by also stressing "can't".

They can't come on Friday.

As you can see from the above example the sentence, "They can't come on Friday" is longer than "They can come on Friday" because both the modal "can't" and the verb "come" are stressed.

So, what does this mean for my speaking skills?

Well, first of all, you need to understand which words we generally stress and which we do not stress. Basically, stress words are considered content words such as

— Nouns e.g. kitchen, Peter

— (most) principal verbs e.g. visit, construct

— Adjectives e.g. beautiful, interesting

— Adverbs e.g. often, carefully

Non-stressed words are considered function words such as

— Determiners e.g. the, a, some, a few
— Auxiliary verbs e.g. don't, am, can, were
— Prepositions e.g. before, next to, opposite
— Conjunctions e.g. but, while, as
— Pronouns e.g. they, she, us

Let's return to the beginning example to demonstrate how this affects speech.

> *The beautiful Mountain appeared transfixed in the distance.* (14 syllables)
>
> *He can come on Sundays as long as he doesn't have to do any homework in the evening.* (22 syllables)

Even though the second sentence is approximately 30% longer than the first, the sentences take the same time to speak. This is because there are 5 stressed words in each sentence. From this example, you can see that you needn't worry about pronouncing every word clearly to be understood (we native speakers certainly don't). You should however, concentrate on pronouncing the stressed words clearly.

Now, do some listening comprehension or go speak to your native English speaking friends and listen to how we concentrate on the stressed words rather than giving importance to each syllable. You will soon find that you can understand and communicate more because you begin to listen for (and use in speaking) stressed words. All those words that you thought you didn't understand are really not crucial for understanding the sense or making yourself understood. Stressed words are the key to excellent pronunciation and understanding of English.

A Diphthongs

The following series of pronunci tion exercises combines words beginning with the same diphthong sound followed by similar diphthong sounds. Voiced and voiceless consonants are paired to help students compare and contrast similar consonant formation.

- Repeat each line slowly, listen for the minor differences between the vowel and consonant sounds.
- Repeat each line three times. Each time repeat more quickly trying to keep the sounds distinct.
- Find a partner and listen to each other repeat the lines.
- Try to invent sentences using each sound at least once. For example: We ate cake and flew a kite on my birthday.
- Don't worry too much about the sentence making much sense!

'ay' as in 'day'	'ai' as in 'die'
bay	buy
pay	pie
day	die
table	tie
gay	guy
cake	kite

say	sigh
zany	Zaire
shape	shy
Jake	jive
chase	child
hey!	hi

□ □□□□□□□□□□

The following E diphthongs are pronounced differently in British and American English. British English drops the 'r' sound and pronounces a slight 'uh' - 'hair' becomes 'hehuh'. In American English the 'r' is strongly pronounced - 'hair' becomes 'hehrrr'.

'ieh(r)' as in 'near'	'ehi(r)' as in 'hair'
beer	bear
peer	pear
dear	dare
tear (drop of water)	tear (rip)
gear	garish
clear	Claire
seer	snare
sheer	share
jeer	Jerry
cheer	chair
here	hair

O Diphthongs

The following series of pronunciation exercises combines words beginning with the same diphthong sound followed by similar diphthong sounds. Voiced and voiceless consonants are paired to help students compare and contrast similar consonant formation.

'ou' as in 'home' 'ow' as in 'house' 'oi' as in 'boy'

bowl bow boy

Pope	pow-wow	poise
don't	Dow	doily
toe	towel	toy
go	gouge	goiter
cope	cow	coy
soap	sour	soy sauce
zone	zowie!	(none)
show	shower	(none)
Jones	jowl	join
chose	ciao!	choice
home	howl	hoist

U Sounding Vowels

The following series of pronunciation exercises combines words beginning with the same consonant sound followed by similar vowel sounds. Voiced and voiceless consonants are paired (b - voiced / p - voiceless, d - voiced / t - voiceless, etc.) to help students compare and contrast similar consonant formation.

'long uh' as in 'put'	'short uh' as in 'up'	'oo' as in 'shoe'
butcher	but	boot
put	pup	poof!

(none)	duck	do
Tokay	tough	tooth
good	gulp	Google
cook	cup	cool
soot	supper	suit
(none)	(none)	zoom
shook	shut	shoot
(none)	jump	June
churn	Chuck	choose
hook	hup!	who

Changing Meaning through Word Stress

When you are speaking English the words you stress can change the underlying meaning a sentence. Let's take a look at the following sentence:

I don't think he should get the job.

This simple sentence can have many levels of meaning based on the word you stress. Consider the meaning of the following sentences with the stressed word in **bold**. Read each sentence aloud and give a strong stress to the word in **bold**:

I don't think he should get the job.

Meaning: *Somebody else thinks he should get the job.*

I **don't** think he should get the job.

Meaning: *It's not true that I think he should get the job.*

I don't **think** he should get that job.

Meaning: *That's not really what I mean.*

OR I'm not sure he get that job.

I don't think **he** should get that job.

Meaning: *Somebody else should get that job.*

I don't think he **should** get that job.

Meaning: *In my opinion it's wrong that he's going to get that job.*

I don't think he should **get** that job.

Meaning: *He should have to earn (be worthy of, work hard for) that job.*

I don't think he should get **that** job.

Meaning: *He should get another job.*

I don't think he should get that **job**.

Meaning: *Maybe he should get something else instead.*

As you can see, there are many different ways this sentence can be understood. The important point to remember is that the true meaning of the sentence is also expressed through the stressed word or words.

Accent Reduction

The main purpose of accent neutralisation/reduction is to help proficient English speakers speak with a more North American or British accent. The main cause of this trend towards accent neutralisation/reduction is the demand created by outsourcing. Outsourcing is generally defined as the transfer of components or large segments of an organisation's internal infrastructure, staff, processes or applications to an external resource. The trend is towards outsourcing to countries where this work can be done at lower cost to the company. One of the most popular countries for outsourcing is India due to its wealth of highly educated English speakers.

Accent neutralisation / accent reduction comes into play when these workers speak to North Americans who have difficulties understanding their accents. Of course, the English spoken is excellent. The problem that arises is that many customers have difficulties understanding accents other than their own, hence accent neutralisation or reduction becomes important for customer satisfaction.

Common Techniques and Goals

Here are some of the common focus areas for accent neutralisation or accent reduction classes:

— Changing speech patterns

— Voice production

— Intonation and rhythm

— Taking on a new North American "Personality" - *I think is a great way to distance oneself from the more distasteful implications of accent reduction*

The stated goals of many of these programmes include:

— Changing regional accents to increase personal and professional opportunities

— Engaging in extensive conversations, presentations, and telephone calls

— Be more confident and effective, both socially and professionally - *This must apply to English speakers living in North America!*

- Improved professional image of your company
- Greater understanding from listeners.

ENGLISH PHONOLOGY

English phonology is the study of the phonology (i.e. the sound system) of the English language. Like all languages, spoken English has wide variation in its pronunciation both diachronically and synchronically from dialect to dialect.

This variation is especially salient in English, because the language is spoken over such a wide territory, being the predominant language in Australia, Canada, Ireland, New Zealand, the United Kingdom and the United States in addition to being spoken as a first or second language by people in countries on every continent.

With no conclusive, internationally recognised standards for English, even the English spoken in different countries can occasionally prove to be an impediment to understanding what is said, although for the most part the different regional accents of English are mutually intelligible.

Although there are many dialects of English, the following are usually used as prestige or standard accents: Received Pronunciation for the UK, General American for the USA and General Australian for Australia. The number of speech sounds in English varies from dialect to dialect, and any actual tally depends greatly on the interpretation of the researcher doing the counting.

The Longman Pronunciation Dictionary by John C. Wells, for example, using symbols of the

International Phonetic Alphabet, denotes 24 consonants and 23 vowels used in Received Pronu-nciation, plus two additional consonants and four additional vowels used in foreign words only.

For General American it provides for 25 consonants and 19 vowels, with one additional consonant and three additional vowels for foreign words. The American Heritage Dictionary, on the other hand, suggests 25 consonants and 18 vowels (including r-colored vowels) for American English, plus one consonant and five vowels for non-English terms.

Phonetic Reduction in Connected Speech

There is phonetic reduction in connected speech, especially in words which have once been focal but have since passed to a lower information status: the first time a word is used, its articulation is more precise and the resulting acoustic signal more distinct than in subsequent tokens of the same word.

'Phonetic' mean that the effect can be described in terms of vocal tract inertia: since the representatives in speech: anything can change to anything else, as long as the change is regular/ predictable, that is, as long as the linkage to the underlying phonemic identity of each item is discoverable. This will allow one-to one, many-to-one, and one-to-many mappings between underlying components and surface components, as well as no mapping.

This type of phonology would look at the sound system of a language as an abstract code in which the identity of each element is determined entirely by its own original description and by its relationship to other elements.

Fudge provides an early example of introducing phonological primes with no implicit phonetic content. Foley's point of view is not unlike this: his thesis is that phonological elements can be identified only through their participation in phonological rules:

> As, for example, the elements of a psychological theory must be established without reduction to neurology or physiology, so too the elements of a phonological theory must be established by consideration of phonological processes, without reduction to the phonetic characteristics of the superficial elements and only when phonology frees itself from phonetic reductionism will it attain scientific status.'

Kelly and Local also take a position of this sort: 'We draw a strict distinction between phonology and phonetics. Phonology is formal and to be treated in the algebraic domain; phonetics is physical and in the temporal domain.'

Any school which determines membership of a phonological class by distribution alone might be said to take a similar stance: de Saussure's analogy between phonological units and pieces in the game of chess could be interpreted this way.

Phonology could be seen as the study of meaning-bearing sound units and their representatives in different environments, regardless of whether they change the meaning, with the addition of constraints as to what sorts of substitutions are likely or even possible. If constraints are specified, phonology offers some insight into why changes take place, based on the articulatory and perceptual properties of the input and output. A congruous assumption is that since vocal tracts, ears, and brains are essentially the same in all humans, some aspects of phonology are universal.

Most currently-favoured phonological theories are like this: in Chomsky's terminology, they attempt to achieve explanatory as well as descriptive adequacy.

Generative grammar opted to incorporate links between abstract phonology and the vocal tract through (1) a choice of features which reflect normal human articulatory possibilities and (2) 'parsimony' (the rule using the fewest features is best, hence rules involve small changes which are easily executed by the vocal tract). Linked to this are the 'natural classes': sounds which are articulated similarly are very likely to undergo similar phonological changes.

Autosegmental phonology achieves a link with the vocal tract through structuring of feature lattices, gestural phonology through encoding phonological elements in terms of the articulators themselves. It is, of course, generally understood that articulatory involvement cannot always be presupposed by a theory because in some cases the physical motivation for a phonological event has become inadequate. For example, the f /v alternation in singular/plural words (shelf /shelves, roof /rooves, loaf /loaves) is not currently productive, though variation owing to this process is still part of the language.

These remains of decommissioned processes are often called fossils. Or the alternation could be the result of an interaction with another linguistic level rather than having an articulatory origin. For example, in the utterance 'I have to wear what I have to wear', the first 'have' can be pronounced while the second cannot, for lexical/syntactic reasons.

These cases aside, when we look at motivated alternations, we begin to consider the relationship between abstract categories and human architecture: this could be seen as a small subset of the mind/body problem so beloved of philosophers.

Most theories of phonology assume that spoken language involves categories which exist only in the minds of the speakers and for which there is thought to be a set of templates: some for segmental categories, some for tones, intonation, and voice quality.

Another assumption which is usually not overt is that in speech production, our goal is to articulate strings of perfect tokens of these categories, but are held back from doing so by either communicative or physical demands. Again musing on logical possibilities, we can imagine several variations on mind-body interaction.

Some sequences take more attention than others, and some even take more attention than they are worth, because they do not contribute substantially to the understanding of the utterance. Over time, it becomes customary to simplify these forms through a kind of unspoken treaty amongst native speakers of a language. This leads to our not pronouncing, say the 't' in 'Christmas', the 'b' in 'bomb', or the 'gh' in 'knight'.

Eventually, the base form starts to be learned as a whole, so that younger speakers of the language do not even know that, for example, 'bomb' has a potential 'b' at the end and find out only by learning to spell.

These changes are primarily matters of convention and history. Articulatory ease is more evidently a cause for change in cases such as word-final devoicing, which occurs very often with English oral obstruents: one rarely encounters a fully voiced final fricative or stop, even in careful speech.

This change from the base form has a different psychological status from the previous one, however: native speakers do not know they are devoicing, and new generations are not led to believe that final obstruents are voiceless, though they pick up the habit of devoicing, as they must in order to sound like native speakers. It is easy to find languages where this feature is an overt convention. It seems that here we have a peaceful settlement between what the vocal tract wants and what the brain decides to do.

Many characteristics of spoken English seem to fall into this intermediate category. For example, in vowel + nasal sequences, it is not unusual to nasalize the vowel and to not execute the closure for the nasal consonant. This means that words like 'can't' can be realised as [kbt]. At the phonetic level, then, there can be a contrast between plain and nasalised vowels in words like 'cart' and 'can't'. While this is a full-fledged phonological process in languages like

French and Portuguese, it is merely a tendency in English and Japanese: a habit which is picked up by native speakers and used subconsciously.

In other cases, vocal tract influences seem clear and inevitable, as in the fronting of velar consonants before front vowels. This is called 'coarticulation' and is a function of the fact that the vocal tract has to execute sequences in which commands can conflict ('front' for [i], 'back' for [k], and a compromise is reached.

This seems to me a clear case of a phonetic process, but it also seems quite clear that it can have phonological consequences, as in Swedish, where the sequence (which was historically and which is still spelled) [ki] is pronounced [çi], or as in English alternations such as act/action. Bladon and Al-Bamerni have also pointed out that resistance to coarticulation can occur as a result of other demands of a language.

In English, [k] and [i] can coarticulate freely, since a fronted [k] is not likely to be misinterpreted. In languages with a [c], [k] has less freedom to move about. This indicates that even process which are largely controlled by the vocal tract can be moderated by cognitive processes.

Resistance to coarticulation can also develop for no obvious reason: in Catalan, there is virtually no nasalisation of vowels before nasal consonants, though it is found in the other Romance languages. Cites denasalisation as a natural process, and we can see this at work elsewhere in Catalan.

What is the difference between saying that changes have to have an articulatory or perception explanation and saying that the vocal tract is responsible for the changes? What is the interaction between the physical demands of the vocal tract and the desire on the part of the speaker to (a) be intelligible and (b) sound like a native speaker? The answer seems obvious: as long as constraints determined by the shape and movement of the vocal tract are included in one's phonology, there is in principle no way to draw a boundary between phonetics and phonology.

Processes which are essentially phonetic (such as nasalisation of vowels before nasal consonants) are prerequisites for certain phonological changes (lack of closure for the nasal consonant, leading to distinctiveness of the nasalised vowel).

Distinctions which are essentially phonological (such as the word-final voicing contrast in English obstruents) are signalled by largely phonetic features such as duration of the preceding vowel (though, granted, this process is exaggerated in English beyond the purely phonetic).

Language features which are said to be phonological are constantly in the process of becoming non-distinctive, while features said to be phonetic are in the process of becoming distinctive. There are obvious cases of truly phonological processes and truly phonetic ones, but between them there is a continuum rather than a definable cutoff point.

FAST SPEECH RULES

Casual speech processes are often referred to as 'fast speech rules'. Results are not yet conclusive about whether increase in speech rate increases the amount of phonological reduction: it seems clear that phonetic undershoot takes place as less time is available for each linguistic unit, but evidence cited below suggests that cognitive factors are more important than inertia, despite the fact that connected speech processes are often called 'fast speech rules'.

A common sense view of connected speech has it that the vocal tract is like any other machine: as you run it faster, it has to cut corners, so the gestures get less and less extreme. Say, for example, you are tracing circles in the air with your index finger.

At a rate of one a second, you can draw enormous circles but if you're asked to do 6 per second, you have to draw much smaller circles, and a rate of 15 per second is impossible, no matter how small they are. So if you try to do 15, you might get only 10 - effectively, 5 have dropped out.

The same reasoning is applied to the vocal tract: as you execute targets faster and faster, the gestures become smaller and smaller, and sometimes they have to drop out entirely, which is why you get deletions in so-called 'fast speech'. A moment's thought will convince you that the analogy here is not very good: the vocal tract is a very complicated device, and different parts of it can move simultaneously. The elements which comprise the vocal tract are of different sizes and shapes and have different degrees of mobility. The speech units which are being produced are very different from each other.

And, most importantly, speech is not just an activity, it is a means of communication. This means that different messages will be transmitted nearly each time a person speaks, different units will be executed in sequence, and different conditions will be in effect to constrain articulation. For example, one can speak to a person who is very close or very far away, to a skilled or unskilled user of the language, with or without background noise.

The 'finger circle' analogy also does not take into account the relationship between the higher centres of the brain and articulation. Speech is a skill which we practise from infancy and one over which we have great control: does it seem likely that anyone would run their vocal tract so fast that not all of the sounds in a message could be executed?

One might imagine singing a song so fast that not all of the notes/words could be included: the difference here is that we are executing a pre-established set of targets with a fixed internal rhythm intended for performance at a certain speed. But presumably, in real speech, our output is tailored to the situation in which it is uttered and has no such constraints.

Another argument against our very simplistic view of 'fast speech deletion' is that there are very distinct patterns of reduction in connected speech, related to type of sound and place of occurrence. If one were simply speaking too fast to include all the segments in a message, would not the last few simply drop out, as with our 'finger circles'? Rather, we find specific types of sounds being under-executed, in predictable locations.

And these 'shortcuts' are different from language to language as well. Surely the importance of cognitive control of these mechanisms cannot be underrated. Lindblom follows this line of reasoning in his 'H&H theory' of speech, which essentially says that in any given situation, the vocal tract will move as little as possible, provided that (situationally-determined) intelligibility can be maintained. This theory thus predicts a limit to the degree of undershoot based on the communicative demands of the moment.

While this point of view has a lot to be said for it, it cannot be considered a phonetic or phonological theory exclusively: it embraces all areas of linguistics, because they all contribute to the 'communicative demands of the moment'.

It is obvious that the types of reduction which we have been looking at also occur in slow speech: if you say 'eggs and bacon' slowly, you will probably still pronounce 'and' as [m], because it is conventional - that is, your output is being determined by habit rather than by speed or inertia. This brings us back full circle to the question 'phonetics or phonology?' Habit and convention are language-specific and are part of the underlying language plan rather than part of moment-to-moment movement of the articulators. Habits of pronunciation are systematic and predictable and can be linked only indirectly to articulator inertia.

SPOKEN ENGLISH IN A BILINGUAL CONTEXT

Spoken English Development Factors

There is no such thing as a homogeneous group of deaf or hard of hearing children. Each child's ability to develop spoken English skills is influenced by a variety of factors. There are two major prerequisites: biological potential and an intrinsic motivation or interest. Factors related to potential and motivation for a deaf or hard of hearing child can be broken down into several specific areas.

These areas include: amount of residual hearing, benefit of amplification, consistency of hearing aid use, language competency, family support, intelligence, and attitude-both of the child and of the family.

Each of these factors plays a complex, interrelated role in the overall development of spoken English skills. No one factor determines the extent to which a deaf or hard of hearing child will develop intelligible spoken English skills. However, factors related to the degree of access the child has to the spoken English model are the most important.

Children with limited access to the auditory part of speech and who are unable to use their hearing to monitor their own speech production have a truly challenging task ahead of them. While there are exceptions, those children with less auditory access to English tend to be less likely to develop functional spoken English skills.

If you have an interest in soccer or the piano, you may want your child to develop skills in these areas also. However, a child who has no natural ability or interest is not likely to develop significant skills. This is not to say that the child should not be encouraged to participate in sports or music, but that it should be done by exposing the child to the skill and encouraging regular but enjoyable practice, then letting the child's own aptitudes and interest determine to what extent this area of interest can realistically be fostered.

Of course, many hearing parents' desire for their child to speak, and their hope for their child to interact easily with the hearing majority cannot be compared to their desire for the child to succeed in a sport. However, there are some very real parallels when looking at the child's intrinsic motivation to learn to speak.

Residual hearing

The acuity of a child's hearing can be objectively measured and documented on an audiogram. However, when discussing auditory skills, it is important to note that an audiogram often does not reflect a child's functional abilities. The audiogram provides information about how well a child can hear "pure tones." It does not indicate how well a child comprehends spoken language within or outside a communicative context.

Amplification

Each child responds differently to amplification. A child's use of hearing aids may or may not provide enough benefit to allow full or even partial access to spoken English. For many children, hearing loss does not just weaken the auditory signal, it distorts sound as well. To use an analogy, hearing aid use can be compared to a radio.

Hearing aids can increase the volume of speech the child is hearing. However, if the incoming signal is full of "static"-in this case, distortion due to damage to the cochlea or auditory nerve-then the hearing aid may have little benefit. Hearing aids can provide more auditory information by increasing the volume, but they do not necessarily increase comprehension of spoken English.

Cochlear implants provide auditory information by directly stimulating the cochlea. Although they may increase awareness of sound, their success rate in contributing to developing oral language skills has been minimal in children who had not already learned spoken English before their hearing loss. It is critical to carefully consider all factors when contemplating irreversible attempts to amplify sound, such as implants.

In the final analysis, it is important to observe a child's behaviour to determine how much benefit he or she is receiving from any form of amplification. It may be safe to assume that consistent use of amplification in meaningful settings for a child who demonstrates benefit from amplification is likely to have impact on his or her spoken English development.

Language competency

One critical factor in speech development is language competency. Deaf children of deaf parents often demonstrate a significant linguistic advantage in spoken English over deaf children of hearing parents. The deaf or hard of hearing child who already understands the world and is fully able to communicate his or her thoughts is more able and willing to learn the skills necessary to develop spoken language skills.

A deaf or hard of hearing child's knowledge of written English can be a valuable tool for developing competence in spoken English. As a deaf or hard of hearing child begins to read, he or she is able to make the connection between the printed and the spoken word, especially if the speech pathologist practices listening and speaking skills with stories or sentences that have meaning for the child while still modeling English structure. This visual reinforcement is very helpful for teaching the sound combinations in new vocabulary.

Written English also provides a way for deaf and hard of hearing children to gain complete access to the structure of the language, providing a clearer model of English syntax than they are likely to get from the spoken signal. Knowing the structure of English is particularly important in speechreading, which involves filling in many gaps by predicting or guessing what cannot be heard or perceived on the lips.

Family Support

Family support is vital not only for speech and language development but for emotional and cognitive development.

A family that accepts their deaf or hard of hearing child and respects the child's visual and linguistic needs will help that child reach his or her maximum potential. Given broad-based support and encouragement, children seem more likely to develop the underlying confidence necessary to become successful communicators. Such children are better equipped to negotiate difficult interactions that may require them to use trial and error in applying a variety of communication strategies.

Intelligence level

A child's intelligence level alone is not a good indicator of ability to develop spoken English. Many intelligent deaf and hard of hearing adults do not develop spoken English skills, despite intense efforts. However, a child with aptitude in certain areas of intelligence may be able to make more sense of the distorted speech he or she perceives or may have greater ability to utilise other contextual cues in the environment.

Young children are naturally inquisitive, and those whose language and cognitive development are supported early tend to view speech as just another interesting thing to learn. Over time, their understanding of the goals and their level of motivation may increase as they begin to see the potential applications in their later lives.

Sign vs. speech

If there are no concrete objective methods to predict the child's potential, then how can one determine whether a very young child will have the ability to develop spoken English skills?.

Currently, sign language is widely used in the education of deaf and hard of hearing children. The effects of this misconception can be devastating to the child's welfare. The opposite view is that a child should be primarily exposed only to sign language and that spoken English skills could be taught after the child has mastered his or her first language.

With these either/or approaches, a child receives exposure to only one language, limiting the potential language development of the child. By placing a child in a bilingual environment that is truly sensitive to spoken language issues, one where the two languages are used in similar contexts but kept separate, parents and teachers have more information to determine what the child is capable of achieving.

Language development is one of the priorities of any early education program. Since access to spoken language is limited for a child who is deaf or hard of hearing, one way to provide full access to language is to use a visual language. Within the school day, as well as in their home environment, the children can also be exposed to spoken English in safe, predictable contexts. In this way they can be exposed to both languages separately during the course of everyday interactions. It then becomes possible to more clearly observe progress in each language, both expressive and receptive. When determining a child's potential to develop spoken English skills, it is important to follow the child's lead-to let the child help us determine where his or her abilities, preferences, and language input needs lie.

Keeping the languages separate allows deaf and hard of hearing children to function like other bilingual children. They are able to make decisions regarding the most appropriate mode to use in a given situation. Keeping the languages separate also helps clinicians and teachers to more accurately assess the intelligibility of the child's speech production without signed cues, and to better observe his or her comprehension of the spoken signal.

In this way, children also begin to get a clearer understanding of when their speech is being understood and when it is not. Approaching the languages as they are-separate languages-enables the children to realistically assess their own abilities in each; it also contributes to overall communicative competency by helping children know when they need to develop alternative strategies.

Realistic expectations

Spoken English development for deaf and hard of hearing children can range from full use of complex structures and varied vocabulary to the use of spoken or mouthed English words limited to specific situations. It is important to understand that, despite what parents may want for their children, not every deaf or hard of hearing child will develop spoken English skills. Some will develop only basic functional skills. Others will be able to engage in a predictable, everyday conversation, but be unable to express or understand complex ideas in spoken English.

Still others will have a fairly full range of oral language knowledge and skills, but will need to work very hard to fully comprehend the subtle nuances of each communication event. Spoken

English simply may not play the same role in the lives of some deaf and hard of hearing speakers that it does for hearing persons. Some important decisions must therefore be made about how much time and energy a child will be asked to devote toward mastering this skill during the course of his or her education.

If too much emphasis is placed on speech development, the child's language and academic skills may suffer, not to mention self-esteem. Although intensive speech therapy may increase a child's articulation skills, it may also result in decreased acdemic performance. The hours of forced speech work that some deaf and hard of hearing children experience may not only take valuable time away from academic work or experiential learning, but leave a lasting emotional impact.

It is natural for parents to want their child to talk. However, it is important to put that desire in perspective and to respect a child's natural abilities and tendencies. It is important for parents to get enough information to recognise the very real effects-especially for a child who has not yet learned language-of not having complete access to the auditory part of speech. In this way, parents can not only contribute valuable insight and information, they can begin to determine for themselves how much spoken English potential their child has.

Bilingual Strategies

In order for any child to become bilingual, it is important that he or she receive meaningful exposure to two languages. For many hearing children, this happens naturally when there are two languages necessary for the child to negotiate his or her environment. However, for most bilingual children, a determined strategy must be implemented to provide full access to at least one language, or the child may be in danger of not fully developing either language.

A number of different strategies can be employed, including designating specific people to use each language, setting specific times that each language is used, using one language in the home and one outside the home, or using both languages interchangeably.

In general, the two strategies that work well are:

1) having specific people use each language, and
2) designating specific times, settings, or circumstances for each language to be used.

In order to illustrate how the first strategy can work, let's look at a class of two- and three-year-olds at a school for the deaf. In this class there are six children, a deaf teacher, and a hearing teacher's assistant. The children come from a variety of backgrounds and have a variety of hearing losses. At center time, the children are free to move around the classroom deciding what activity they want to participate in. They may participate in such activities as the sand table, building blocks, or the dramatic play area. The teacher and the assistant interact with different children throughout the classroom.

The teacher has just finished playing with two students who are placing blocks one on top of the other and knocking them down when the speech-language therapist joins the class. The therapist-the designated spoken English model-goes over to the students and begins to play with them. As the blocks fall down she says "uh-oh" using visual and/or tactile cues to encourage the children to imitate these sounds.

One of the children knocks down the blocks again and approximates "uh-oh." The therapist later moves to another area where a little boy is playing with a doll. The boy puts the doll down and says "baby." The therapist responds by saying "the baby is sleeping." "Sleep," copies the boy. A little later at the water table, the therapist makes her voice go from high to low as she pours water into a container.

As you can see in this example, the strategy used is to have two people using the two different languages. The children learn that the speech-language therapist is presenting auditory information and this information can be individually geared to the receptive and expressive skills of each child. Interacting with the children in the classroom is often easiest with children of this age. A therapist can move around the room and engage children in activities that interest them and are tailored to their abilities. This also allows the teacher and therapist many opportunities to observe the children using both languages in natural contexts.

As children become older, strategy two may be utilised more, as it maybe less disruptive to bring children to a separate area or room to work on spoken English. During these separate times, the therapist would be primarily using spoken English with sign explanations or visual cues as necessary.

At home parents could also use the second strategy by setting aside specific times or predictable parts of each day to work on spoken English skills with their child.

As the children move into the pre-kindergarten and elementary years, there are three general groups depending on how much access they have to spoken English. In one group are the children who develop spoken English skills that, on the surface, appear similar to those of hearing children. Their auditory skills, with hearing aids, are sufficient to allow them quite a bit of access to spoken English.

The needs of these children are very different from the needs of another group, which consists of children whose auditory access to English is more limited. They depend on speechreading, other visual cues, and tactile information to learn spoken English skills.

The children in this second group do not naturally acquire speech skills; rather these skills must be taught, and the children will acquire them to varying degrees. Yet another group of children, due to profound deafness or some disability, will not easily develop any substantive spoken English skills. Time and effort are better spent developing speechreading and general communication skills.

These groups are distinctive not only in the way they develop spoken English skills but also in the way they will use these skills. Although they all share the goal of developing their communicative competence to their utmost potential, each of these groups requires a different strategy for presenting spoken English.

6

Improve Workplace Communication Skills

There are a few tricks to making a vernacular accent more globally understandable.

- Try making sure that 'air' comes out of your mouth when saying the letters, 'T, P, K' and the sound 'Ch'.
- Focus on elongating your vowel sounds. This will also automatically slow down your rate of speech.
- Sing English songs out loud!
- Watch news shows on channels like CNN and BBC.
- The web site www.m-w.com is great for pronunciation help.
- Buying books on pronunciation and language that come with audio cassettes.

SPRUCE UP YOUR WRITING SKILLS

- Well-written magazines, like The Economist and India Today, are great to read not only to improve language skills but also to learn more about the world.

— In terms of books, read what interests you.

The basic goal is to read as much as you can.

There are a plethora of good authors who are popular today. Some good writers whose language is easy to follow include Vikram Seth, Jhumpa Lahiri, Paulo Coelho, J D Salinger, Albert Camus and Roald Dahl. People tend to forget basic grammar when writing e-mails. An e-mail is nothing more than a letter which is sent electronically. Make sure salutations and content are professional. Use special phrases when attaching documents. For example, "Please find attached with this e-mail a report on..." This helps you sound professional.

Five Exercises

i. Pretend you are a newscaster and read out the newspaper to your mirror.

ii. Do not read local newspapers. Focus on national newspapers.

iii. While reading a book, underline all the words you do not know. Look them up in the dictionary.

iv. Make a list of these words, and make sure you use at least five of them in a conversation during the day.

v. Most important, make an effort to speak in English to your friends and family.

CRASH COURSE IN COMMUNICATION

Talking is easy; communication, which means an exchange or communion with another, requires greater skill. An exchange that is a communion demands that we listen and speak skilfully, not just talk mindlessly. And interacting with fearful, angry, or frustrated people can be even more difficult, because we're less skilful when caught up in such emotions. Yet don't despair or resign yourself to a lifetime of miscommunication at work or home! Good communicators can be honed as well as born. Here are a few tips to get you started.

- Don't take another person's reaction or anger personally, even if they lash out at you in what seems a personal manner. Another person's mood or response is more likely about fear or frustration than it is about you as an individual. Take a deep breath and count to 10, and see it as a way of letting the other person vent before he is able to communicate what's really on his mind.
- You don't have to have all the answers. It's OK to say, "I don't know." If you want to find out, say so, then follow up to share your findings. Or you may decide to work on the problem together to find the answer.
- Respond (facts and feelings); don't react (feelings) – e.g., "Tell me more about your concern" or "I understand your frustration" instead of "Hey, 'm just doing my job" or "It's not my job" (which is sure to cause more irritation). Share responsibility for any communication in which you're a participant, and realise that sometimes, maybe often, your own personal reactions may be causing your frustrations about communicating with others.

— Understand that people want to feel heard more than they care about whether you agree with them. It's strange how many people complain about others not hearing them, yet they don't listen to others either! You can show that you're listening by giving someone your complete attention and saying things like:

"Tell me more about your concern."

"What is it about XXX that concerns you?"

"I'm interested in what you've just said. Can you share a little bit about what lead you to that belief?"

"What would have to happen for you to be more comfortable with XXX?"

— Remember that what someone says and what we hear can be amazingly different! Our personal filters, assumptions, judgments, and beliefs can distort what we hear. Repeat back or summarise to ensure that you understand. Restate what you think you heard and ask, "Have I understood you correctly?" If you find yourself responding emotionally to what someone said, say so, and ask for more information: "I may not be understanding you correctly, and I find myself taking what you said personally. What I thought you just said is XXX; is that what you meant?"

— Acknowledge inconvenience or frustration and offer a timeline, particularly if you need someone else's cooperation or your activities will affect them.

— Look for common ground instead of focusing solely on differences. What might you both be interested in (e.g., making the experience as nondisruptive as possible)? One way to begin discovering commonality is to share your underlying intention – for example, "My intention in sharing this is to help you succeed on this project."

- Remember that change is stressful for most people, particularly if your activities affect them in a way that they aren't scheduling or controlling. Our routines can be comforting in the midst of what appears to be a chaotic world. So if you're in someone's space or need him to do something on your timeline, provide as much information as you can about what you'll need from the person and when. If you can, tell him how what you're doing will benefit him.
- Work to keep a positive mental focus. One of the choices we always have is how we see or experience any given circumstance. Many people who are considered skilful and successful, including professional athletes and cultural leaders, work to maintain a positive mind-set. Ask yourself, "What's great about this?" or "What can I learn from this?" to help maintain a positive state. Don't forget to adopt a variety of stress reduction practices that work best for you.
- Understand that most people, including you, have a unique, often self-serving, agenda. This isn't necessarily bad, because it helps us achieve and protect ourselves. Just don't assume that someone will know or share your agenda, so talking about what's most important to you and asking what's most important to others, can help build a solid foundation for conversation.

- Improve your listening skill. Most people think they listen well, but the truth is that most of people don't listen at all – they just speak and then think about what they're going to say next. Good listening often means asking good questions and clearing your mind of distractions, including what you're going to say next, whom you're meeting with next, or what's going on outside. When someone makes prickly comments or complaints, there's often a concern or fear lurking. Like a detective, ask questions that get to the bottom of someone's real concern or agenda. Only then can you have a truly rich, beneficial conversation.

TIPS FOR MASTERFUL COMMUNICATION

- *Watch your language.* You may use metaphors to offer something your audience can relate to – a common thought or feeling. But many leaders rely on battle metaphors or violent, divisive language such as "Let's conduct guerrilla warfare," or "obliterate the competition." These metaphors reinforce win-lose, self-interested behavior rather than collaboration. Even many sports metaphors have become empty cliches. Opt for clear, positive language and straightforward sincerity to foster shared understanding and earn the support of your group.
- *Follow through.* Failure to follow through on rhetoricaccounts for no small amount of the cynicism and weariness seen in today's workplace. If you make a promise, follow

through with action, even if the action ends up being an explanation of why the promise can't be enacted. Also, don't contradict your rhetoric by, for example, talking about great customer service while treating fellow colleagues arrogantly or rudely.

— *Deal with uncertainty*. Don't be afraid to talk about failure, midcourse adjustments, or "bugs" that the organisation must work through. Create the expectation that these will be a normal part of organisational life. You'll be telling the truth. Throughout a transition, clearly communicate the context of what it means and why decisions were made (goals, reasons, participants, estimated effects, costs, etc.).

— *Be an active listener*. Good listening is an art too few people have mastered. Concentrate on the speaker's message, and resist distractions. Keep an open mind to others' ideas. Don't tune out if you disagree. Indicate you understand what the speaker said by reframing key points: "Let me be sure I understand correctly. You're saying?"

— *Manage conflict*. Identify and involve major stakeholders. Hold one-on-one or very small group discussions early to vent anger. Make sure that everyone knows in advance why meetings are called. Set ground rules that create an "attack-free," safe haven for dialogue. Use nonjudgmental, noninflammatory language like "I perceive?" or "It seems to me?" Reiterate that personal attacks and blame aren't constructive. Identify and reiterate common ground or common goals; focus on areas of agreement.

Don't force a resolution; it's OK to agree to disagree.

- *Respond, don't "re-act."* We often "re-act" to others based on something that happened to us before. Responding mindfully rather than re-acting emotionally requires self-knowledge and discipline, but it allows us to be more effective in our communication. As a leader, you're a role model - you set the tone for what's appropriate in the organisation. Reflect on your hot buttons, and identify a "keep calm" strategy for when they get pushed.
- *Give feedback.* Many of us soften feedback - at the expense of clarity - to avoid confrontation. Provide specific examples that illustrate your critique. For example, instead of "Your attitude is bad" or "That just didn't work," say, "When you miss deadlines, then cross your arms and look away when I talk with you, it gives me the impression you don't care about the quality of your work. Can you help me understand this differently?" Don't forget positive feedback; studies show that a high percentage of employees rarely receive positive feedbackfrom their manager.
- *Invite participation.* Hold meetings that include employees from different areas, and encourage everyone to contribute. Ask employees to send you e-mail regarding their ideas for doing things more effectively, and respond to all queries. Have a "graffiti wall" where employees and leaders can exchange concerns and ideas. This will provide the group with different

perspectives of the issues discussed and help ensure the top-down/bottom-up information flow.

- *Keep your team up-to-date.* Let employees know how their efforts compare to their performance goals and how they are supporting the total picture. Be honest; communicate bad news as well as good news.
- *Connect personally with employees.* Since someemployees may not have frequent contact with you, create opportunities to do so. Sincere face-to-face interaction is key; it gives more weight to telephone, e-mail, or print communications between meetings.
- *Take advantage of communication resources.* Studies show that the most successful entrepreneurs and leaders know their limitations and seek outside counsel and resources.

POWERFUL QUESTIONS

Questions can be one of the most effective communication tools available to us. Strong relationships, strategic plans, award-winning collateral, and the meaningful exchange of ideas and information are all products of asking skilful questions. If they're not, your communications could be weak or worthless, and you may experience miscommunications more often than necessary. Why is the ability to ask skilful questions so powerful? Questions are the means we use to excavate new information, to compare our perspective with reality, and to learn more about what others are thinking and perceiving. When we don't ask questions, we're assuming that we know everything there is to know about the subject or the person. Is this ever the case? Rarely.

Power of Questions

- *Interpersonally*— Asking questions demonstrates that you're listening (and actually helps you to listen), which always helps to strengthen relationships. Think of a conversation when someone didn't ask you a single question. How did you feel? What perception did you have of that person? Would you want to interact with him or her in the future? By setting a goal to ask several questions in all of your interactions, you'll gain powerful information to improve your own performance, strengthen relationships, and reduce misunderstandings.
- *Intrapersonally* — Many personal-mastery practices include the process of asking self-directed questions to determine your most fulfilling journey. As the philosophers-of-old emphasized, only the "examined life" is worth living. After all, if you don't ask yourself, how will you "know thyself?" Yet this isn't as easy to do as it is to say, particularly in Western cultures where people will do just about anything to avoid being quiet and focusing inward. Silence can be unnerving in our busy, noise culture — yet quiet reflection is the fertile ground that yields insightful questions and responses.
- *Suspending assumptions* — Inquiry is a key element of dialogue, which encourages us to suspend assumptions to more fully understand

another person's perspective. In day-to-day interactions, assumptions often lead to miscommunications, mismatched expectations, stress, damaged relationships, or unfulfilled responsibilities. The simple act of clarifying and confirming what you understand to be true, and seeing if others have a similar understanding, can eliminate the negative consequences of making too many assumptions. To do this, ask questions that ensure you have a common understanding of what is being discussed, and of what action needs to be taken. For example, the seemingly obvious question, "Will you take care of that?" would ensure that someone is taking responsibility for an action item, and that no two people are doing the same task. On an interpersonal level, checking in with someone about his intention to send a memo or about a comment that you perceived as rude or unsettling can help foster mutual understanding and unearth your own assumptions that may cause you to be overly sensitive.

— *Communicating clearly* — Any unasked (and thus, unanswered) question, is a trap door waiting to open under your feet. For example, imagine not asking a client what her desired outcome is. How will you reach a goal that you don't know about? Internally, consider a team whose members advocate ideas, but don't take the time to understand others' ideas or bring discussions to closure. The length and frequency of their meetings can soar, while actual progress creeps along at a snail's pace. Take time to ask thoughtful questions of each person. This is also a tremendous way to demonstrate your respect for each person and his ideas, which boosts morale and can increase employees' contributions to the business.

- *Working more effectively* – When teammates, leaders, and managers have the information that they need to do their jobs best, the enterprise benefits from increased productivity, and individuals reap the rewards of high morale and low stress (both are products of having, rather than hoarding, information). How do these constituents get the information they need? By asking. First of all, most people can't read others' minds. So the information won't come if not solicited. Secondly, it is the individual's responsibility to ask for what's needed; no one else should manage this.

Asking skilful questions requires much more than putting a question mark at the end of a thought. First, you must make a habit of actually asking questions – as opposed to stating your ideas, opinions, feedback, etc. Second, you have to raise your awareness of when questions can (or could have) helped improve an interaction, even if it went well.

Use these exercises to flex, build and hone your skilful-questioning aptitude:

- *Ask before advocating*. In your next meeting or conversation, try to ask a sincere, relevant question before advocating your point – in every instance. The topic of your questions might include gathering more information, clarifying a statement or perspective that someone shared, or asking for other participants' thoughts. Be sure to notice how the tenor of the meeting changes, and how people respond (actually and behaviourally).

- *Examine past assumptions.* Think of an instance when you or someone else made an assumption, and when the outcome of the interaction was poor or less than ideal. Write down at least five questions you could have asked during that interaction to prevent assumptions from being made.
- *Inquire, don't interrogate.* Thoughtful questions are a powerful tool for learning more and fostering understanding, yet no one likes to be interrogated! As with any other communication tool, be aware of your own intention for asking the question (e.g. learning more versus attacking someone else's idea), as well as the tone of your voice, body language, and word choice.
- *A step you can take right now.* Identify at least three opportunities you have in the next week to practice using inquiry and probing questions.

What' s striking are the reasons why people continuously lie (or choose not to speak truthfully) - especially when there are communication tools that allow each of to us be skilfully honest and respectful.

Some of the reasons people choose to lie include the desire to:

- Avoid conflict,
- Avoid someone else' s anger or hurt,

- Avoid hurting someone' s feelings,
- Diminish someone else or make them feel bad,
- Feel more worthy of admiration and respect,
- Gain power,
- Avoid having to face an unpleasant truth about themselves,
- Avoid admitting mistakes, and
- Keep "the boat from rocking", hoping everything will pass over, unnoticed.

Interestingly, it' s possible that the intention behind telling a lie might on occasion be well-meaning, although often ego or self-centeredness are at the root. Regardless, it' s how the intention is executed that' s unacceptable, or that results in a strained relationship and a high-stress mindset.

Can you be skilfully honest in these situations? Often times, yes, and yet it takes work and continual, deliberate practice. The following exercises and approaches to help break any pattern of avoiding the truth that you have established, allowing you to opt for respectful, authentic communication.

Mindset-adjustment tips

- When a person lies, it' s a decision that he or she has made as to how the situation should be handled; assuming that a person is not mentally ill, lying is a choice often made out of a lack of skilfulness. If you haven' t already, recognise the power - and result - of this self-will and these choices.

- For people who have created a habit of lying, the first course of action toward skilful honesty is to shift your mindset. Lying is often a "survival mode" created in childhood or early life, so requires the care, gentleness and perseverance needed to deconstruct a destructive habit and replace it with a healthier, more skilful one.
- *Understand when and why you lie* What triggers your decision-making process to discern that a lie is the best route? What fear is behind this choice? For instance, your fear of being wrong, or that you' ll be perceived as being unlikeable or cruel if you speak truthfully, or a fear that you lack the skill to speak the truth in a kinder, more respectful way that may be better received by someone else. In any particular situation, why do you believe that the lie will have the better outcome, and for whom?
- *Use your knowledge to fend off poor decision-making*: Fully examine and assess your answers to the above questions. Once your motivation for lying is unearthed, you' ll be better equipped to recognise your tendencies when they appears and to tackle inclinations to lie.
- *Explore all options before acting or reacting*: Lying can be the product of a snap-decision, made in haste without thoughtful consideration. When you sense yourself crafting a lie, take a pause. Ask your "audience" if you might take a moment to consider the issue or question at hand, if you need time to collect your thoughts.

During this thinking time, review the question or comment, your motivations and intentions.

These grounding techniques give you the opportunity to make a wiser choice in responding and build your confidence for doing so.

TIPS FOR COMMUNICATING CHANGE

While organisational change requires more than 10 tips, here are 10 key things to keep in mind when planning, announcing, implementing, and communicating a change initiative:

- *Remember that there's no one perfect way to communicate change.* Change is uncomfortable, and adapting to change is messy. The perfect Gantt chart does not a painless change experience make. Why? Because tasks are easy to list, but behavior and long-held habits are not easy to change. Gather outside information, solicit perspectives, and adapt the approaches for your organisation and group.
- *Start by asking yourself what exactly is changing and why.* Too many programmes are heavy on the jargon and light on the substance of what the buzz phrases mean in the day-to-day reality of the organisation' s people. You have to make that link. For example, what does it mean when you say the organisation needs to be more responsive? What behaviours characterise a so-called flat organisation? Go to the root of what you're trying to achieve from an organisational behavior perspective, and give the jargon life.
- *Know what results you want, ideally, from both the*

change initiative and the communication programme or tactic. What's the call to action for the communication programme? What's the call to action for the specific communication tactic? What systemic or operations changes are under way that provide the framework for the desired results and behaviours?

— *Include communication strategists at the very beginning of the discussions about the change, on the strategic team from the start.* Too often, qualified communicators are involved after backlash is in full force, when the leaks and rumour mills are rampant.

— *Share information with employees as soon as possible.* There's a real dilemma in public companies, where investor communication is a priority and employees hear about a merger or reorganisation on their car radio while commuting to work. Once fear and insecurity are heightened, you waste a lot of time getting back to a place of order, understanding, and productivity, and many people head for their desks to update resumes and to call employment recruiters.

— Keep in mind that quantity is fine, but quality and consistency are crucial. Most managers are quoted as saying, "You can't communicate too much," but you can communicate too much insignificant or insensitive information. You can't communicate too much significant, substantial information.

— *Longevity.* Remember that a change effort starts with the announcement or a merger or change initiative. Many leaders and managers underestimate the length of time required by a change cycle.

— *Remember to use a variety of communication pathways and vehicles.* Some organisations make an enormous mistake in using only one vehicle, such as e-mail or the company intranet site. Redundancy and repetition are helpful in creating an effective communication programme.

PRESENTATION

Powerful Presentations

Important presentations are intimidating. Whether it's an informal lunch appointment or a stand-up-in-front-of-a-room-full-of-blue-suited-business people meeting, you know you've got a lot riding on what you say and how you say it. The following are the few presentation skills:

— *Create rapport.* Usually the most important thing your prospect is sizing up is YOU. While you're busily focused on the substance of your presentation, they're figuring out whether you're the kind of person they can work with and trust. So relax a little and create a personal connection.

— *Get to your important points right away.* Even if you don't prepare a formal presentation, don't let the discussion wander. Be very clear about your key points and get to them. You don't want to leave the meeting kicking yourself for having forgotten to mention the one thing you know could get you the job.

- *Be prepared.* You not only have to be prepared about what you're going to say, you need to research your audience.
- *Practice.* Not only should you practice your presentation a number of times before you ever do one "live," but you should schedule your least likely prospects first. Use those presentations as "practice" to learn to sharpen your message and skills.
- *Don't assume they've read anything.* No matter what you've sent to people ahead of time, they probably won't have read it or had it sink in.
- *Have answers prepared.* Before you go, anticipate as many possible questions and have clear concise answers ready. That way, you won't be flustered. "I'm glad you asked that," you can reply, and then launch into your prepared response.
- *Know what questions you won't answer.* Some things shouldn't be discussed in a first meeting or in a large group, and you should have an answer ready to deflect those questions.
- *Set a follow-up.* Don't leave a meeting without a clear statement of what will happen next. It's okay to say, "So, what's the next step?" Don't expect them to suggest the next step; they may be looking to you for leadership.. You may need to decide on a deadline ahead of time to give the process a sense of closure.

BUSINESS ENGLISH SPEAKING SKILLS

Widely regarded as the language of international

business, English is essential to today's commercial environment, both for companies seeking to trade overseas and for employees wishing to develop careers in global industries.

Register Usage

Register use is one of the most important aspects of correct English usage for advanced users of the language. In other languages (French, German, Italian, etc.) formality can be signalled through the formal / informal "you" (du - Sie, tu - Vous, tu - Lei, etc.). In English, register is a key element in expressing degrees of formality.

Here is an overview of registers with specific examples for specific occasions.

- *Register*: Type of language used when speaking to others
- *Vertical Register*: Language used varying in degrees of formality
- *Horiznta1 Register*: Jargon, slang, etc. used in communicating with your friends, colleagues, etc.

Language Registers

- *Frozen* - Language that does not change - Prayers and pledges, "set" speech which is often scripted
- *Formal* - Complete sentences and specific word usage. - Formal English often used to show respect used in places such as work, school and public offices
- *Consultative* - Formal register used in conversation - colleagues, peers, etc

— *Casual* - Language used in conversation with friends. - idiomatic and often full of slang, used to signal belonging to a given group

— *Intimate* - Language between lovers (and twins). - "private" language full of codewords only known to the two

Here are four examples of different situations using different types of language to express similar sentiments:

Job Interview Questions and Answers

The job interview in English contains specific questions and appropriate answers. It also requires a certain flexibility in your usage of tenses. This feature provides tips on job interview questions and answers in English. When you walk in the room the very first impression you make on the interviewer can have a great influence on the rest of the interview. It is important that you introduce yourself, shake hands, and are friendly. The first question is often a "breaking the ice" (establish a rapport) type of question. Don't be surprised if the interviewer asks you something like:

— How are you today?

— Did you have any trouble finding us?

— What do you think of the weather lately?

Don't be surprised by the friendly tone. The interviewer wants to put you at ease (help you relax). Answer the question without going into too much detail. The language you use should be simple but polite, for example;

- How are you today?
  - GOOD
  - I'm fine thank you, and you
  - I'm well thank you.
  - BAD
  - So, so
- OK
- Not so well

Talking About Experience Qualifications

Talking about your experience and credentials (qualifications) is the most important part of any job interview. Your qualifications include your education from High School on and any special training you may have done in the past. Your experience is any work that you have done that is directly or indirectly related to the job you are applying for.

Education

Remember that your education took place in the past. Therefore you need to use the past tenses, for example:

- I attended the University of Helsinki from 1987 to 1993.
- I graduated with a degree in agricultural planning. Etc.
- If you are currently a student you should use the following present tenses:
  - I am currently studying at the University of New York and will graduate with a degree

in Economics in the spring.

– I am studying English at the Borough Community College.

Remember to include any training you may have had when talking about your education. This includes any computer training, correspondence courses, etc. Make sure to mention your English studies. This is very important as English is not your first language and the employer may be concerned about this fact. Assure the employer that you are continuing to improve your English skills by any courses you may be taking, or by saying that you study a certain number of hours a week to improve your skills.

Experience and qualifications

Work experience is by far the most important topic of any job interview (at least in the United States and Britain). Therefore, it is important to explain what experience you have in detail. Generally, employers want to know exactly what you did and how well you accomplished your tasks. This is not the time to be modest. Be confident, and talk freely about your accomplishments in past employment.

When talking about current employment be careful to use the present perfect or present perfect continuous. This signals that you are still performing these tasks at your current job, for example:

Smith and Co. have employed me for the last 3 years as a salesperson.

I have been creating customer contacts for 6 months.

When talking about past employers use the past tenses to signal that you are no longer working for that company, for example:

> I was employed by Jackson's from 1989 to 1992 as a clerk.
>
> I worked as a receptionist at the Ritz while I was living in New York.

Talking about responsibilities

Most importantly, you will need to demonstrate your qualifications and skills, which are required for the job you are applying for. The job skills that you have acquired in the past may not have been for the same exact job. Therefore, it is important to show how the capabilities you do have relate to the job you are applying for.

Essential Job Interview Tips and Tricks

This section focuses on some of the common questions that are asked during the interview and appropriate responses to these questions.

Interviewer: Tell me about yourself.

Candidate: I was born and raised in Milan, Italy. I attended the University of Milan and received my master's degree in Economics. I have worked for 12 years as a financial consultant in Milan for various companies including Rossi Consultants, Quasar Insurance and Sardi and Sons. I enjoy playing tennis in my free time and learning languages.

Candidate: I've just graduated from the University of Singapore with a degree in

Computers. During the summers, I worked as a systems admini-strator for a small company to help pay for my education.

Comment: This question is meant as an introduction. Do not focus too specifically on any one area. The above question will often be used to help the interviewer choose what h/she would like to ask next. While it is important to give an overall impression of who you are, make sure to concentrate on work related experience. Work related experience should always be the central focus of any interview (work experience is more important than education in most English speaking countries).

Interviewer: What type of position are you looking for?

Candidate: I'm interested in an entry level (beginning) position.

Candidate: I'm looking for a position in which I can utilise my experience.

Candidate: I would like any position for which I qualify.

Comment: You should be willing to take an entry level position in an English speaking company as most of these companies expect non-nationals to begin with such a position. In the United States, most companies provide many opportunities for growth, so don't be afraid to start from the beginning!

Interviewer: Are you interested in a full-time or part-time position?

Candidate: I am more interested in a full-time position. However, I would also consider a part-time position.

Comment: Make sure to leave open as many possibilities as possible. Say you are willing to take any job, once the job has been offered you can always refuse if the job does not appeal (not interest) to you.

Interviewer: Can you tell me about your responsibilities at your last job?

Candidate: I advised customers on financial matters. After I consulted the customer, I completed a customer inquiry form and catalogued the information in our database. I then collaborated with colleagues to prepare the best possible package for the client. The clients were then presented with a summarised report on their financial activities that I formulated on a quarterly basis.

Comment: Notice the amount of detail necessary when you are talking about your experience. One of the most common mistakes made by foreigners when discussing their former employment is to speak too generally. The employer wants to know exactly what you did and how you did it; the more detail you can give the more the interviewer knows that you understand the type of work. Remember to vary your vocabulary when talking about your responsibilities. Also, do not begin every sentence with "I". Use the passive voice, or an introductory clause to help you add variety to your presentation

Interviewer: What is your greatest strength?

Candidate: I work well under pressure. When there is a deadline (a time by which the work must be finished), I can focus on the task at hand (current project) and structure my work schedule well. I remember one week when I had to get 6 new customer reports out by Friday at 5. I finished all the reports ahead of time without having to work overtime.

Candidate: I am an excellent communicator. People trust me and come to me for advice. One afternoon, my colleague was involved with a troublesome (difficult) customer who felt he was not being served well. I made the customer a cup of coffee and invited both my colleague and the client to my desk where we solved the problem together.

Candidate: I am a trouble shooter. When there was a problem at my last job, the manager would always ask me to solve it. Last summer, the LAN server at work crashed. The manager was desperate and called me in (requested my help) to get the LAN back online. After taking a look at the daily backup, I detected the problem and the LAN was up and running (working) within the hour.

Comment: This is not the time to be modest! Be confident and always give examples. Examples show that you are not only repeating words you have learned, but actually do possess that strength.

Interviewer: What is your greatest weakness?

Candidate: I am overzealous (work too hard) and become nervous when my co-workers are not pulling their weight (doing their job). However, I am aware of this problem, and before I say anything to anyone, I ask myself why the colleague is having difficulties.

Candidate: I tend to spend too much time making sure the customer is satisfied. However, I began setting time-limits for myself If I noticed this happening.

Comment: This is a difficult question. You need to mention a weakness that is actually a strength. Make sure that you always mention how you try to improve the weakness.

Interviewer: Why do you want to work for Smith and Sons?

Candidate: After following your firms progress for the last 3 years, I am convinced that

Smith and Sons are becoming one of the market leaders and I would like to be part of the team.

Candidate: I am impressed by the quality of your products. I am sure that I would be a convincing salesman because I truly believe that the Atomizer is the best product on the market today.

Comment: Prepare yourself for this question by becoming informed about the company. The more detail you can give, the better you show the interviewer that you understand the company.

Interviewer: When can you begin?

Candidate: Immediately.

Candidate: As soon as you would like me to begin.

Comment: Show your willingness to work!

The above questions represent some of the most basic questions asked on any job interview in English. Probably the most important aspect of interviewing in English is giving detail. As a speaker of English as a second language, you might be shy about saying complicated things. However, this is absolutely necessary as the employer is looking for an employee who knows his or her job. If you provide detail, the interviewer will know that you feel comfortable in that job. Don't worry about making mistakes in English. It is much better to make simple grammar mistakes and provide detailed information about your experience than to say grammatically perfect sentences without any real content.

Common Interview Questions

First impressions

The first impression you make on the interviewer can decide the rest of the interview. It is important that you introduce yourself, shake hands, and be friendly and polite. The first question is often a "breaking the ice" (establish a rapport) type of question. Don't be surprised if the interviewer asks you something like:

- How are you today?
- Did you have any trouble finding us?
- Isn't this great weather we're having?

This type of question is common because the interviewer wants to put you at ease (help you relax). The best way to respond is in a short, friendly manner without going into too much detail. Here is some examples correct responses:

Interviewer: How are you today?

You: I'm fine, thank you. And you?

OR

Interviewer: Did you have any trouble finding us?

You: No, the office isn't too difficult to find.

OR

Interviewer: Isn't this great weather we're having?

You: Yes, it's wonderful. I love this time of year.

Interviewer: Did you have any trouble finding us?

You: No, the office isn't too difficult to find.

Here are some examples of incorrect responses:

Interviewer: How are you today?

You: So, so. I'm rather nervous actually.

OR

Interviewer: Did you have any trouble finding us?

You: As a matter of fact it was very difficult. I missed the exit and had to return via the highway. I was afraid I was going to be late for the interview.

OR

Interviewer: Isn't this great weather we're having?

You: Yes, it's wonderful. I can remember this time last year. Wasn't it awful! I thought it would never stop raining!

Interviewer: Did you have any trouble finding us?

You: No, the office isn't too difficult to find.

Getting down to business

Once the pleasant beginnings have finished, it's time

to begin the real interview. Here are a number of the most common questions that are asked during the interview. There are two examples of excellent replies given for each question. Following the examples, you will find a comment describing the type of question and important things to remember when answering that type of question.

Interviewer: Tell me about yourself.

Candidate: I was born and raised in Milan, Italy. I attended the University of Milan and received my master's degree in Economics. I have worked for 12 years as a financial consultant in Milan for various companies including Rossi Consultants, Quasar Insurance and Sardi and Sons. I enjoy playing tennis in my free time and learning languages.

Candidate: I've just graduated from the University of Singapore with a degree in Computers. During the summers, I worked as a systems administrator for a small company to help pay for my education.

Comment: This question is meant as an introduction. Do not focus too specifically on any one area. The above question will often be used to help the interviewer choose what h/she would like to ask next. While it is important to give an overall impression of who you are, make sure to concentrate on work related experience. Work related experience should always be the central focus of any interview.

Interviewer: What type of position are you looking for?

Candidate: I'm interested in an entry level (beginning) position.

Candidate: I'm looking for a position in which I can utilise my experience.

Candidate: I would like any position for which I qualify.

Comment: You should be willing to take an entry level position in an English speaking company as most of these companies expect non-nationals to begin with such a position. In the United States, most companies provide many opportunities for growth, so don't be afraid to start from the beginning!

Interviewer: Are you interested in a full-time or part-time position?

Candidate: I am more interested in a full-time position. However, I would also consider a part-time position.

Comment: Make sure to leave open as many possibilities as possible. Say you are willing to take any job, once the job has been offered you can always refuse if the job does not appeal (not interest) to you.

Interviewer: Can you tell me about your responsibilities at your last job?

Candidate: I advised customers on financial matters. After I consulted the customer, I completed a customer inquiry form and catalogued the information in our database. I then collaborated with colleagues to prepare the best possible package for the client. The clients were then presented with a summarised report on their financial activities that I formulated on a quarterly basis.

Comment: Notice the amount of detail necessary when you are talking about your experience. One of the most common mistakes made by foreigners when discussing their former employment is to speak too generally. The employer wants to know exactly what you did and how you did it; the more detail you can give the more the interviewer knows that you understand the type of work. Remember to vary your vocabulary when talking about your responsibilities. Also, do not begin every sentence with "I". Use the passive voice, or an introductory clause to help you add variety to your presentation

Interviewer: What is your greatest strength?

Candidate: I work well under pressure. When there is a deadline, I can focus on the task at hand and structure my work schedule well. I remember one week when I had to get 6 new customer reports out by Friday at 5. I finished all the reports ahead of time without having to work overtime.

Candidate: I am an excellent communicator. People trust me and come to me for advice. One afternoon, my colleague was involved with a troublesome customer who felt he was not being served well. I made the customer a cup of coffee and invited both my colleague and the client to my desk where we solved the problem together.

Candidate: I am a trouble shooter. When there was a problem at my last job, the manager would always ask me to solve it. Last summer, the LAN server at work crashed. The manager was desperate and called me in to get the LAN back online. After taking a look at the daily backup, I detected the problem and the LAN was up and running within the hour.

Comment: This is not the time to be modest! Be confident and always give examples. Examples show that you are not only repeating words you have learned, but actually do possess that strength.

Interviewer: What is your greatest weakness?

Candidate: I am overzealous and become nervous when my co-workers are not pulling their weight. However, I am aware of this problem, and before I say anything to anyone, I ask myself why the colleague is having difficulties.

Candidate: I tend to spend too much time making sure the customer is satisfied. However, I began setting time-limits for myself If I noticed this happening.

Comment: This is a difficult question. You need to mention a weakness that is actually a strength Make sure that you always mention how you try to improve the weakness.

Interviewer: Why do you want to work for Smith and Sons?

Candidate: After following your firms progress for the last 3 years, I am convinced that Smith and Sons are becoming one of the market leaders and I would like to be part of the team.

Candidate: I am impressed by the quality of your products. I am sure that I would be a convincing salesman because I truly believe that the Atomizer is the best product on the market today.

Comment: Prepare yourself for this question by becoming informed about the company. The more detail you can give, the better you show the interviewer that you understand the company.

Interviewer: When can you begin?

Candidate: Immediately.

Candidate: As soon as you would like me to begin.

Comment: Show your willingness to work!

The above questions represent some of the most basic questions asked on any job interview in English. Probably the most important aspect of interviewing in English is giving detail. As a speaker of English as a second language, you might be shy about saying complicated things. However, this is absolutely necessary as the employer is looking for an employee who knows his or her job. If you provide detail, the interviewer will know that you feel comfortable in that job.

Don't worry about making mistakes in English. It is much better to make simple grammar mistakes and provide detailed information about your experience than to say grammatically perfect sentences without any real content.

Bibliography

Beckson, Karl, and Arthur Ganz. *Literary Terms: A Dictionary*, 3rd ed. New York: Farrar, 1989.

Corbett, Edward P. J. *Classical Rhetoric for the Modern Student*. 4th ed. New York: Oxford UP, 1999.

Crowley, Sharon, and Debra Hawhee. *Ancient Rhetorics for Contemporary Students*, 2nd ed. Boston: Allyn & Bacon, 1999.

Cuddon, J. A. *A Dictionary of Literary Terms and Literary Theory*. Oxford: Blackwell, 1991.

Epsy, Willard R. *The Garden of Eloquence: A Rhetorical Bestiary*. New York: Harper, 1983.

Frew, Robert, Richard Guches, and Robert Mehaffy. *Writer's Workshop*. Palo Alto, California: Peek Publications, 1984.

Garner, Bryan A., ed. *The Oxford Dictionary of American Usage and Style*. New York: Oxford UP, 2000.

Goldstein, Norm, ed. *The Associated Press Stylebook and Briefling on Media Law*, 41st ed. New York: Associated P, 2006.

Greenbaum, Sidney. *The Oxford English Grammar*. New York: Oxford UP, 2006.

Harmon, William, and C. Hugh Holman. *A Handbook to Literature*, 8th ed. Upper Saddle River: Prentice-Hall, 2000.

Herrick, James A. *The History and Theory of Rhetoric: An Introduction*. Boston: Allyn & Bacon, 2005.

Hollander, John. *Rhyme's Reason: A Guide to English Verse*, 3rd ed. New Haven: Yale UP, 2001.

Lanham, Richard A. *Analyzing Prose*, 2nd ed. New York: Continuum, 2003.

_______________ *A Handlist of Rhetorical Terms: A Guide for Students of English Literature*. 2nd ed. Berkeley: U of California P, 1991.

Lewis, Norman. *Instant Spelling Power*. New York: Amsco College Publications, 1976.

Makaryk, Irena R., ed. *Encyclopedia of Contemporary Literary Theory: Approaches, Scholars, Terms.* Toronto: U of Toronto P, 1993.

McArthur, Tom, ed. *The Oxford Companion to the English Language.* New York: Oxford UP, 1992.

Norton, Sarah, and Brian Green. *The Bare Essentials, Form B.* Toronto: Holt, Rinehart and Winston of Canada, Limited, 1988.

Sloane, Thomas O., ed. *Encyclopedia of Rhetoric.* New York: Oxford UP, 2001.

Strunk, William, and E. B. White. *The Elements of Style.* New York: Macmillan Publishing Co., Inc., 1972.

Sullivan, Tony. *Grammar.* Cambridge: The National Extension College, 1979.

Vickers, Brian. *Classical Rhetoric in English Poetry.* Carbondale: Southern Illinois UP, 1970.

Woodson, Linda. *A Handbook of Modern Rhetorical Terms.* Urbana: NCTE, 1979